DEATH
and
DIGNITY

DEATH
and
DIGNITY

MAKING CHOICES
AND TAKING CHARGE

Timothy E. Quill, M.D.

W. W. Norton & Company
New York • London

The text of this book is composed in 11.5/14 Simoncini Garamond
with the display set in Berkeley Old Style Medium.
Composition and manufacturing by The Haddon Craftsmen, Inc.
Book design by Chris Welch.

Permission is granted for the preface by the *New England Journal of
Medicine* for the use of Timothy E. Quill, M.D., "Death and Dignity: A
Case of Individualized Decision Making" (*NEJM*, 1991; 324:691–94).

Permission is granted for the letter which appears on p. 214 by the *New
England Journal of Medicine* for the use of correspondence by Stewart A.
King, M.D., "Death and Dignity: The Case of Diane" (*NEJM*, 1991;
325:658).

Permission is granted for the first half of Chapter 8 by the *New England
Journal of Medicine* for the use of Timothy E. Quill, M.D., Christine
Cassel, M.D., and Diane Meier, M.D., "Care of the Hopelessly Ill:
Potential Clinical Criteria for Physician-Assisted Suicide" (*NEJM*, 1992;
327:1380–84).

Library of Congress Cataloging-in-Publication Data
Quill, Timothy E.
Death and dignity : making choices and taking charge / Timothy E.
Quill.
p.   cm.
Includes bibliographical references and index.
1. Terminal care. 2. Assisted suicide. I. Title.
R726.8.Q55 1993
362.1'75—dc20   92-20710

ISBN 0-393-31140-6

W. W. Norton & Company, Inc.
500 Fifth Avenue, New York, N.Y. 10110
W. W. Norton & Company Ltd.
10 Coptic Street, London WC1A 1PU
1 2 3 4 5 6 7 8 9 0

To Diane

CONTENTS

PREFACE

DEATH AND DIGNITY

A Case of Individualized Decision Making*

D iane was feeling tired and had a rash. A common scenario, though there was something subliminally worrisome that prompted me to check her blood count. Her hematocrit was 22, and the white-cell count was 4.3 with some metamyelocytes and unusual white cells. I wanted it to be viral, trying to deny what was staring me in the face. Perhaps in a repeated count it would disappear. I called Diane and told her it might be more serious than I had initially thought—that the test needed to be repeated and that if she felt worse, we might have to move quickly. When she pressed for the possibilities, I reluctantly opened the door to leukemia. Hearing the word seemed to make it exist. "Oh, shit!" she said. "Don't tell me that." Oh, shit! I thought, I wish I didn't have to.

Diane was no ordinary person (although no one I have ever come to know has been really ordinary). She was raised in an alcoholic family and had felt alone for much of her life. She had

*Reprinted from the *New England Journal of Medicine,* 324:691–694 (March 7), 1991.

vaginal cancer as a young woman. Through much of her adult life, she had struggled with depression and her own alcoholism. I had come to know, respect, and admire her over the previous eight years as she confronted these problems and gradually overcame them. She was an incredibly clear, at times brutally honest, thinker and communicator. As she took control of her life, she developed a strong sense of independence and confidence. In the previous 3½ years, her hard work had paid off. She was completely abstinent from alcohol, she had established much deeper connections with her husband, college-age son, and several friends, and her business and her artistic work were blossoming. She felt she was really living fully for the first time.

Not surprisingly, the repeated blood count was abnormal, and detailed examination of the peripheral-blood smear showed myelocytes. I advised her to come into the hospital, explaining that we needed to do a bone marrow biopsy and make some decisions relatively rapidly. She came to the hospital knowing what we would find. She was terrified, angry, and sad. Although we knew the odds, we both clung to the thread of possibility that it might be something else.

The bone marrow confirmed the worst: acute myelomonocytic leukemia. In the face of this tragedy, we looked for signs of hope. This is an area of medicine in which technological intervention has been successful, with cures 25 percent of the time—long-term cures. As I probed the costs of these cures, I heard about induction chemotherapy (three weeks in the hospital, prolonged neutropenia, probable infectious complications, and hair loss; 75 percent of patients respond, 25 percent do not). For the survivors, this is followed by consolidation chemotherapy (with similar side effects; another 25 percent die, for a net survival of 50 percent). Those still alive, to have a reasonable chance of long-term survival, then need bone marrow transplantation (hospitalization for two months and whole-body irradiation, with complete killing of the bone marrow, infectious complications, and the possibility for graft-versus-host disease—with a survival of approximately 50 percent, or 25 percent of the original group). Though hematologists may argue over the exact percentages, they don't argue about the outcome of no treatment—certain death in days, weeks, or at most a few months.

Believing that delay was dangerous, our oncologist broke the news to Diane and began making plans to insert a Hickman catheter and begin induction chemotherapy that afternoon. When I saw her shortly thereafter, she was enraged at his presumption that she would want treatment, and devastated by the finality of the diagnosis. All she wanted to do was go home and be with her family. She had no further questions about treatment and in fact had decided that she wanted none. Together we lamented her tragedy and the unfairness of life. Before she left, I felt the need to be sure that she and her husband understood that there was some risk in delay, that the problem was not going to go away, and that we needed to keep considering the options over the next several days. We agreed to meet in two days.

She returned in two days with her husband and son. They had talked extensively about the problem and the options. She remained very clear about her wish not to undergo chemotherapy and to live whatever time she had left outside the hospital. As we explored her thinking further, it became clear that she was convinced she would die during the period of treatment and would suffer unspeakably in the process (from hospitalization, from lack of control over her body, from the side effects of chemotherapy, and from pain and anguish). Although I could offer support and my best effort to minimize her suffering if she chose treatment, there was no way I could say any of this would not occur. In fact, the last four patients with acute leukemia at our hospital had died very painful deaths in the hospital during various stages of treatment (a fact I did not share with her). Her family wished she would choose treatment but sadly accepted her decision. She articulated very clearly that it was she who would be experiencing all the side effects of treatment and that odds of 25 percent were not good enough for her to undergo so toxic a course of therapy, given her expectations of chemotherapy and hospitalization and the absence of a closely matched bone marrow donor. I had her repeat her understanding of the treatment, the odds, and what to expect if there were no treatment. I clarified a few misunderstandings, but she had a remarkable grasp of the options and implications.

I have been a longtime advocate of active, informed patient choice of treatment or nontreatment, and of a patient's right to die with as much control and dignity as possible. Yet there was something about her giving up a 25 percent chance of long-term survival in favor of almost certain death that disturbed me. I had seen Diane fight and use her considerable inner resources to overcome alcoholism and depression, and I half expected her to change her mind over the next week. Since the window of time in which effective treatment can be initiated is rather narrow, we met several times that week. We obtained a second hematology consultation and talked at length about the meaning and implications of treatment and nontreatment. She talked to a psychologist she had seen in the past. I gradually understood the decision from her perspective and became convinced that it was the right decision for her. We arranged for home hospice care (although at that time Diane felt reasonably well, was active, and looked healthy), left the door open for her to change her mind, and tried to anticipate how to keep her comfortable in the time she had left.

Just as I was adjusting to her decision, she opened up another area that would stretch me profoundly. It was extraordinarily important to Diane to maintain control of herself and her own dignity during the time remaining to her. When this was no longer possible, she clearly wanted to die. As a former director of a hospice program, I know how to use pain medicines to keep patients comfortable and lessen suffering. I explained the philosophy of comfort care, which I strongly believe in. Although Diane

understood and appreciated this, she had known of people lingering in what was called relative comfort, and she wanted no part of
it. When the time came, she wanted to take her life in the least
painful way possible. Knowing of her desire for independence and
her decision to stay in control, I thought this request made perfect
sense. I acknowledged and explored this wish but also thought
that it was out of the realm of currently accepted medical practice
and that it was more than I could offer or promise. In our discussion, it became clear that preoccupation with her fear of a lingering death would interfere with Diane's getting the most out of the
time she had left until she found a safe way to ensure her death. I
feared the effects of a violent death on her family, the consequences of an ineffective suicide that would leave her lingering in
precisely the state she dreaded so much, and the possibility that a
family member would be forced to assist her, with all the legal and
personal repercussions that would follow. She discussed this at
length with her family. They believed that they should respect her
choice. With this in mind, I told Diane that information was
available from the Hemlock Society that might be helpful to her.

A week later she phoned me with a request for barbiturates for
sleep. Since I knew that this was an essential ingredient in a
Hemlock Society suicide, I asked her to come to the office to talk
things over. She was more than willing to protect me by participating in a superficial conversation about her insomnia, but it was
important to me to know how she planned to use the drugs and to
be sure that she was not in despair or overwhelmed in a way that
might color her judgment. In our discussion, it was apparent that
she was having trouble sleeping, but it was also evident that the
security of having enough barbiturates available to commit suicide
when and if the time came would leave her secure enough to live
fully and concentrate on the present. It was clear that she was not
despondent and that in fact she was making deep, personal connections with her family and close friends. I made sure that she
knew how to use the barbiturates for sleep, and also that she knew

the amount needed to commit suicide. We agreed to meet regularly, and she promised to meet with me before taking her life, to ensure that all other avenues had been exhausted. I wrote the prescription with an uneasy feeling about the boundaries I was exploring—spiritual, legal, professional, and personal. Yet I also felt strongly that I was setting her free to get the most out of the time she had left, and to maintain dignity and control on her own terms until her death.

The next several months were very intense and important for Diane. Her son stayed home from college, and they were able to be with one another and say much that had not been said earlier. Her husband did his work at home so that he and Diane could spend more time together. She spent time with her closest friends. I had her come into the hospital for a conference with our residents, at which she illustrated in a most profound and personal way the importance of informed decision making, the right to refuse treatment, and the extraordinarily personal effects of illness and interaction with the medical system. There were emotional and physical hardships as well. She had periods of intense sadness and anger. Several times she became very weak, but she received transfusions as an outpatient and responded with marked improvement of symptoms. She had two serious infections that responded surprisingly well to empirical courses of oral antibiotics. After three tumultuous months, there were two weeks of relative calm and well-being, and fantasies of a miracle began to surface.

Unfortunately, we had no miracle. Bone pain, weakness, fatigue, and fevers began to dominate her life. Although the hospice workers, family members, and I tried our best to minimize the suffering and promote comfort, it was clear that the end was approaching. Diane's immediate future held what she feared the most—increasing discomfort, dependence, and hard choices between pain and sedation. She called up her closest friends and asked them to come over to say goodbye, telling them that she would be leaving soon. As we had agreed, she let me know as well.

When we met, it was clear that she knew what she was doing, that she was sad and frightened to be leaving, but that she would be even more terrified to stay and suffer. In our tearful goodbye, she promised a reunion in the future at her favorite spot on the edge of Lake Geneva, with dragons swimming in the sunset.

Two days later her husband called to say that Diane had died. She had said her final goodbyes to her husband and son that morning, and asked them to leave her alone for an hour. After an hour, which must have seemed an eternity, they found her on the couch, lying very still and covered by her favorite shawl. There was no sign of struggle. She seemed to be at peace. They called me for advice about how to proceed. When I arrived at their house, Diane indeed seemed peaceful. Her husband and son were quiet. We talked about what a remarkable person she had been. They seemed to have no doubts about the course she had chosen or about their cooperation, although the unfairness of her illness and the finality of her death were overwhelming to us all.

I called the medical examiner to inform him that a hospice patient had died. When asked about the cause of death, I said, "acute leukemia." He said that was fine and that we should call a funeral director. Although acute leukemia was the truth, it was not the whole story. Yet any mention of suicide would have given rise to a police investigation and probably brought the arrival of an ambulance crew for resuscitation. Diane would have become a "coroner's case," and the decision to perform an autopsy would have been made at the discretion of the medical examiner. The family or I could have been subject to criminal prosecution, and I to professional review, for our roles in support of Diane's choices. Although I truly believe that the family and I gave her the best care possible, allowing her to define her limits and directions as much as possible, I am not sure the law, society, or the medical profession would agree. So I said "acute leukemia" to protect all of us, to protect Diane from an invasion into her past and her body, and to continue to shield society from the knowledge of the degree of suffering that people often undergo in the process of dying. Suffering can be lessened to some extent, but in no way eliminated or made benign, by the careful intervention of a competent, caring physician, given current social constraints.

Diane taught me about the range of help I can provide if I know people well and if I allow them to say what they really want. She taught me about life, death, and honesty and about taking charge and facing tragedy squarely when it strikes. She taught me that I can take small risks for people that I really know and care about. Although I did not assist in her suicide directly, I helped indirectly to make it possible, successful, and relatively painless. Although I know we have measures to help control pain and lessen suffering, to think that people do not suffer in the process of dying is an illusion. Prolonged dying can occasionally be peaceful, but more often the role of the physician and family is limited to lessening but not eliminating severe suffering.

I wonder how many families and physicians secretly help patients over the edge into death in the face of such severe suffering. I wonder how many severely ill or dying patients secretly take their lives, dying alone in despair. I wonder whether the image of Diane's final aloneness will persist in the minds of her family, or if they will remember more the intense, meaningful months they had together before she died. I wonder whether Diane struggled in that last hour, and whether the Hemlock Society's way of death by suicide is the most benign. I wonder why Diane, who gave so much to so many of us, had to be alone for the last hour of her life. I wonder whether I will see Diane again, on the shore of Lake Geneva at sunset, with dragons swimming on the horizon.

The Genesee Hospital
Rochester, NY 14607   TIMOTHY E. QUILL, M.D.

ACKNOWLEDGMENTS

Diane's family has been courageous and generous in allowing me to publicly share their struggle and pain so that others will hopefully suffer less and have more options in the future. Unfortunately, they have had to bear a large proportion of the burden of this process. I hope that they find some satisfaction in the more open exploration that is now occurring in part as a result of Diane's story.

During my legal difficulties, I was supported and sustained by my family, close friends, patients, practice partners, colleagues, office staff, and staff at The Genesee Hospital in countless ways. The leadership within the American College of Physicians and the Society of General Internal Medicine took the risk of expressing public support when there was doubt about the outcome of the grand jury investigation. So many reached out to me with a kind word, a letter of support, a story, or a hug that it would be impossible to thank everyone by name. I especially want to acknowledge those who shared moving personal stories about facing death with someone they loved deeply who was suffering with no relief in sight. These stories helped me stay focused on why I

originally wrote the article, and helped keep my own legal problems in perspective. Many of the ideas and the passions in this
book were fueled by these stories.

Penny Townsend-Quill, my loving wife and partner, has been
my most honest and direct editor, and also a source of unending
support and encouragement. Diane Meier and Chris Cassel have
been wonderful collaborators in the development of the criteria
presented in Chapter 8, and also thoughtful readers and editors of
the manuscript. Marcia Angell of the *New England Journal of Medicine* has been a challenging, courageous editor, who facilitated the
publication of the articles reproduced in the preface and in Chapter 8. Marc LaForce, my boss and good friend, has been a continuing source of guidance, support, and editorial suggestions. Maria
Milella worked tirelessly, organizing responses to the thousands of
phone calls and inquiries that came in the wake of my original
article, and has also helped in editing and proofreading the manuscript. My editor, Amy Cherry of W. W. Norton, has been a
thoughtful, sensitive guide through the process of publication.
Finally, Chuck Sims provided a helpful legal review.

I feel that I am a very lucky person to be connected to and
associated with so many creative, compassionate people. I have
felt honored, sustained, stimulated, and less vulnerable because of
their support and encouragement.

INTRODUCTION

Diane's request for assurance that she would not have to die a lingering death was a defining moment for me as a physician and as a person. As Diane's personal physician, I had to be as open as possible to her fears and concerns about death, and to help her understand and ultimately face the challenges that lay ahead. Diane had seen the ravages of physical, intellectual, and emotional deterioration that can accompany dying, and it terrified her. Though she didn't like, want, or ask for any of the treatment options available to a person with acute leukemia, she eventually understood them fully. Given her restricted choices, her main goal was to stay at home as long as her life had meaning, and then to die as gently and quickly as possible. When she requested my assistance in ensuring a controlled death should her suffering become intolerable, I had to look within myself to see if helping Diane die on her own terms would violate my own personal values or standards. I also had to balance the potential professional and legal repercussions of indirectly assisting her with my own commitment to allowing a dying patient to control her fate as much as possible.

My desire to increase the options available to dying patients is driven largely by my clinical experience. I believe that the care of the dying is one of our highest callings as physicians—as important as healing or curing. Some of my most profound and challenging experiences have been trying to help dying patients maintain dignity, control, and comfort through the terminal stages of their complex illnesses. Many times their journey has taken me outside of well-described medical experience, and far outside of my own personal experience. For example, before I met Diane, I had thought about but never personally faced the question of physician-assisted suicide. I had indirectly helped many patients to die by stopping life-sustaining treatment, or by treating pain with high doses of narcotic pain relievers, but I had never assisted anyone to commit suicide. By listening to and learning from Diane, I found her request to be consistent with the most important values that underlie the care of the dying—values of informed personal choice, minimizing suffering, and nonabandonment.

The process that Diane, her family, and I went through together has had a profound effect on me. I now have a much deeper and more personal appreciation of what might be possible between doctor and patient under such adverse circumstances. Diane lived as fully as possible for the three months from her diagnosis to her death. During that time she received care at home on a hospice program. Her symptoms were managed effectively and she made strong connections with her family and friends. Because she had the potential of an effective escape, her remaining life was not contaminated by the fear that death would become agonizing to her at the end.

My intention in publishing the article reproduced as the preface to this book was to challenge the medical profession to take a more personal, in-depth look at end-of-life suffering. Previously published cases involving physician-assisted deaths were either anonymous or so extreme that they could be relatively easily dismissed by the medical profession. Consideration of the issue by medical ethicists tended to be abstract and intellectual, minimizing the anguish faced by many dying patients and their families. From my work as a hospice consultant and as a personal physician, I knew that untreatable suffering prior to death is unfortunately not rare. I also knew from confidential discussions that other physicians have secretly assisted patients of their own to die under similar circumstances. Being a physician in the established academic mainstream of medicine, I believed that my presentation of this real experience would be difficult for the profession to dismiss. Given the compelling nature of Diane's request, I felt that the article illustrated as much about careful, patient-centered decision making as it did about the physician's potential role in compassionately assisting death.

After the article was published, I received an unwanted education as to how our legal system both works and doesn't work, and how it is influenced by political forces. Although I intended to challenge the profession of medicine, I underestimated the extent to which the general public and the legal system would become interested and involved. Diane's identity was eventually discovered. Her family and I were harassed by the media and enmeshed in the criminal justice system. Diane's body, which she had generously donated to science, was located and subjected to an unwanted, meaningless autopsy to confirm the presence of a lethal amount of medication. The criminal charges considered against me ranged from tampering with public records to manslaughter, and endless newspaper articles recited the potential outcome (though remote) of fifteen years in jail. The case was finally presented to a grand jury, which determined that my actions did not warrant prosecution. The New York State Health Department also reviewed the case; it subsequently found no evidence of professional misconduct and recommended that the New York State Task Force on Life and the Law review the overall subject.

Although I have several misgivings about how the legal investigation unfolded and was to some extent driven by the media, the only regret I have about the care which I gave to Diane herself is that she was alone at her death. The case was dismissed by the grand jury in part because of this tragic fact. Diane had requested to be by herself at the end, but I believe she did so to protect her family and me from potential prosecution should her act be discovered. Diane was a brave person who faced death squarely, but it violates every principle of humane care of the dying if she felt she had to be alone at the end because of our laws. As a physician, I make a solemn promise to my dying patients that I will not abandon them no matter where their illness may take them. Ironically, had I been with Diane at her death, the outcome of the grand jury hearing might have been different.

In the aftermath of my article, I have received over two thousand remarkable letters, many of which contained moving personal stories. People I had known as friends or as patients for years now told me of their experiences, as well as their hopes and fears about their own death. Many who had anguished over the death of a beloved friend or family member now felt that they could share with me what had previously been kept secret. Indignity at the end of life has touched so many, and the stories are so plentiful and profound, that I now believe the problem to be deeper and more common than I originally anticipated. I also believe that if change is to occur, it will be driven by the stories and passions of these witnesses. Firsthand experience with such tragedy makes one more fearful of a difficult death, and also wary of a profession that does not openly acknowledge or respond to its possibility.

Such witnesses know that simple rules, restrictions, and abstract principles do not protect them from the agonizing effects that incurable illness sometimes has on patients and their families and friends. In subsequent chapters, I will use stories from my own personal experience and from letters and conversations to illustrate principles and problems in caring for the terminally ill. I hope that these real-life stories will help us realize that we can no longer turn our backs on such potential indignity at the end of life. It is the stories that provide this book with life and meaning, and keep it focused on real experience. I have attempted to render them accurately, while protecting confidentiality. They have a chilling similarity—I hope many of them will not have to be repeated.

End-of-life suffering has been lessened considerably in the last two decades by the development and broad application of a philosophy of "comfort care" for the dying. Comfort care is a humane approach to medical care that can help provide a dignified, tolerably pain-free, meaningful death for most patients. "Hospice care," "palliative care," and "comfort care" are roughly synonymous terms used to capture this philosophy of treatment, which emphasizes the relief of physical discomfort, and careful attention to the patient's psychological, social, and spiritual needs. As medical director for a hospice program for eight years, I have a profound respect for the ability of comfort care to humanize the care of the dying when it is offered early enough, and applied with skill and compassion. Physicians are becoming more skilled and knowledgeable about palliative care, and society is beginning to allocate more resources to hospice care, yet there still remains a lot to be done to ensure adequate access and effective application.

But end-of-life suffering is not exclusively a problem of access to good palliative care. Unfortunately, some patients still experience anguishing deaths in spite of heroic efforts by skilled physicians, nurses, and family members. Some of the disturbing stories about patients who desperately hoped for death came from families whose relatives had been in formal hospice programs. When physicians and hospice workers shy away from acknowledging the limitations of comprehensively applied comfort care, it devalues the experience of those who have suffered, and frightens those who have been witnesses. In Chapters 4 and 5, both the potentials and the limitations of comfort care are considered in more depth.

While I am an enthusiastic advocate of comfort care, I am

deeply troubled by our profession's unwillingness openly to acknowledge its limitations. If we don't admit to the possibility of
intolerable end-of-life suffering, how are we ever going to explore
alternatives that will respond to the real needs of patients who
have only death to look forward to? This borders on abandoning
those whose need is greatest, and it violates fundamental principles of comfort care for the dying.

If we decide as a society that physicians should not directly
respond to incurably ill patients who request assistance in dying as
the only escape from their suffering, then we must develop alternatives that do not include the denial of the problem, the need for
covert agreements, or abandonment. Medical care must become
more personal, intimate, informed, and individualized. If we open
ourselves to the experiences and requests of people who are
dying, we can then help the medical profession become more
attentive to human suffering and begin to explore more humane
options for all of us at the end of life.

For those who have been witnesses, I hope you feel that this
book acknowledges your experience, and gives you hope that a
broader range of options will become available in the future.
Those who have not personally witnessed difficult deaths may be
alarmed by some of the stories and ideas contained in subsequent
chapters. My intent is not to frighten people, but to inform them
of what can happen if they don't take an active role in their own
medical care. Taking an active role means developing a fully informed philosophy about the end of your life, then ensuring that
your doctor understands it, and that he or she will respect your
health-care decisions and keep you fully informed. It also means
completing a Living Will or selecting a Health Care Proxy (see
Chapter 10), so that someone is empowered to advocate on your
behalf should you lose the mental capacity to make your own
decisions in the future. Your Health Care Proxy must be fully
informed of your philosophy about health care at the end of life,
since his or her job is to try to help make decisions on your behalf
using *your* values and beliefs.

Some of you may want to get involved in the political process whereby our laws and public policy are reconsidered to allow dying patients and their doctors a broader range of options. Such options should never be an alternative to comfort care, but rather become available only when and if comfort care becomes ineffective. Though we may not want to contemplate this possibility, unfortunately it can occur. Under such tragic circumstances, continued meaningless existence with no escape can become the enemy, and death can be a welcome friend. It is true that even with carefully constructed safeguards, there will be risks in formally sanctioning physicians to help such patients to die, just as there are risks in maintaining current prohibitions. We must balance both the risks and the benefits carefully as we consider moving forward. By exploring our hopes and fears about our own death, and by listening and learning from the stories about those who have directly faced death, we will hope to learn how to use medicine's power judiciously to achieve two of its most important objectives: prolonging a meaningful life and humanizing the process of dying.

DEATH
and
DIGNITY

Chapter 1

EARLY BRUSHES WITH DEATH

Formative Experiences as a Resident and Grandson

As medical students and residents in the 1970s, we often made life-and-death decisions about patients without consulting or informing them. Almost all of our hospitalized patients, except those who were facing imminent death, received everything that medical technology had to offer. Occasionally we would independently decide that a patient's prognosis or his quality of life was so poor that we would stop invasive procedures and not perform cardiopulmonary resuscitation at the time of death. Prior to formal "do-not-resuscitate" laws and policies requiring informed consent, patients and families were only rarely given a choice in these matters. The designation for withholding full technological intervention was kept on a chalkboard in the nurses' station, and then penciled into the chart, so that all traces could be eliminated when the patient died or was discharged.

Today, such practices would not be tolerated. Patients are better informed and given the opportunity for more choice about all medical interventions, including cardiopulmonary resuscitation (though perhaps more in theory than in practice). Yet, in the past, when doctors made medical decisions based exclusively on disease-oriented statistics and ignored the personal aspects of care, it almost made sense. Doctors were using medicine and technology to fight disease and ultimately death—a noble battle that we would occasionally even win. The true victories were exhilarating, and the patients who could leave and go on about their lives were so grateful that we, as physicians, would sometimes feel we possessed Godlike powers. Yet there were also more ambiguous victories: patients who emerged from severe illness as shadows of their former selves, often dependent on the technology that helped save them and the health-care system to support and take care of them. If you could remain focused on the disease and the technology, and stay emotionally distant from the devastation of the person, this prolongation of life could almost seem like success.

There were much darker moments—moments when we continued to apply invasive medical technology to prolong life for patients who were already suffering severely, and had only death to look forward to. The motivation behind these treatments was more often the physician's lack of understanding about or acceptance of alternative approaches, and his or her inability to communicate with the patient or family about a poor prognosis, than any malicious intent. As long as one stayed on the surface emotionally, it was far easier to continue technological intervention in a heroic struggle to prolong life than to address the complex and troubling issue that the patient was dying, or that the burden of the medical treatments far outweighed any potential benefit.

"Do you want us to do everything for your father?" Of course the answer is yes, but the meaning of "everything" was poorly understood. The physician, the patient, and the family—each perhaps for different reasons—silently colluded to avoid directly confronting the fact that the patient was not only dying but suffering profoundly in the process. The avoidance of these difficult exchanges can have dire consequences when advanced medical technology stands in the wings, ready to prolong life at all costs, even if it means prolonging a painful death.

FIGHTING WITH DEATH AS
A MEDICAL RESIDENT

In the Emergency Department, sometimes the pace is so fast and the experiences so intense that they almost defy description. In an unpredictable way, one sees the best and worst of society, the best and worst of medicine, and the best and worst of oneself. Even in Rochester, New York, which is a relatively affluent city, several weeks in the Emergency Department will expose any health-care provider to the violence, abuse, brutality, and neglect that exist in our society. In addition to being confronted with patients' overwhelming social and personal problems, some also enter with life-threatening medical emergencies in which the physician's skill can mean the difference between life and death. Medical students and residents, many of whom have had little medical experience outside of the classroom, are sent into this intense environment in order to learn about acute medical care. There they rapidly develop their technological skills, and, in the interest of their emotional survival, they learn to ignore or minimize the overwhelming personal suffering and social problems of the patients they see.

One day in my training, when I was the senior resident in charge of the Emergency Department, made a lasting impression on me. At age twenty-seven, with four years of medical school and eighteen months of residency under my belt, I was feeling reasonably confident about my medical skills. On this particular day, three separate cardiac arrest patients came under my care.

The first patient was a fifty-five-year-old man who was having a heart attack. His father had died of a heart attack in his mid-fifties, and this man was terrified that he too was dying. As we were rapidly trying to relieve his pain and anxiety, and initiate treatment for his heart, he experienced a cardiac arrest from ventricular fibrillation (chaotic electrical activity of the heart that does not pump blood). We immediately went into our highly structured medical protocol and cardioverted him (a painful electrical shock to the chest which can "restart" the heart). His heart rhythm and blood pressure returned. But he awoke even more terrified than before, now with a sore chest from the shock to accompany his heart attack pain, only to have another cardiac arrest. We again cardioverted him, and he again woke up pleading with us not to hurt him and not to let him die. We started more medicines to prevent the ventricular fibrillation and to treat his heart attack, but his heart stopped again and again. Each time he awoke, he implored us to stop hurting him—a plea which we tried to acknowledge, but had to ignore in the interest of saving his life. After electrically shocking him over fifteen times, and trying a series of traditional medications according to our protocol that unfortunately were not working, we started an experimental drug that finally stabilized his heart rhythm, and transferred him to the coronary care unit.

This man subsequently described the terror he felt during his experience in the Emergency Department. He felt attacked, and totally out of control. He wondered if we knew what we were doing. He thought he might literally have died and arrived in Hell. But he also expressed his profound gratitude to us for saving his life, for using the technology of medicine in a knowledgeable and effective way, for not giving up when things looked dismal, and for not giving in to his pleas not to hurt him anymore. This man subsequently went home from the hospital and lived for many years in a full, productive, and satisfying way. If asked about the potential of medical technology to prolong life, I am sure he would be an ardent supporter.

This, we felt, was what medicine was all about. Working on this patient (I say "on" rather than "with" because to stay focused on the job of prolonging his life in the face of his severe suffering during cardiopulmonary resuscitation, we had to depersonalize the process) left us feeling exhilarated and powerful. That one saved life made up for many deaths, and the personal suffering that had been ignored and minimized in so many other patients now seemed justified in the interest of this lofty purpose. Maybe sometimes we really can cheat death and, in this case at least, medical technology scored an exhilarating victory.

Later that same day, we received a call from an ambulance that there was a "medical 500" on the way; ambulance technicians were performing cardiopulmonary resuscitation en route to the hospital. The patient was a sixty-year-old woman with diabetes—nothing else was known. When she arrived, she had no pulse, no blood pressure, and no electrical activity in her heart. We began our protocol, inserting tubes in her lungs, arteries, veins, and bladder, giving her intravenous medicines, and electrically shocking her heart. Because she was a large woman, our chest compressions had to be particularly forceful to keep blood circulating. It was a bloody, brutal resuscitation that continued for over thirty minutes. Finally, after connecting an electrical pacemaker to her heart, we got a heartbeat and her blood pressure returned.

Maybe we really do have Godlike powers, I thought. Maybe if we apply medical technology vigorously and intelligently enough, we really can beat death. As the euphoria started to swell once more, I began a neurological examination on the patient. Her pupils did not react, and inside her eyes were signs of brain swelling. My heart sank as I realized that her heart had survived but her brain had not. Reluctantly I began to arrange for transfer to the intensive-care unit when her family arrived. As I explained to the family what had happened, and tried to help them make sense out of what they now faced, I realized again just how ambiguous and uncertain medicine often is. Though far from impotent, physicians' powers are human and very capable of doing harm as well as good.

Yet we had given this woman a chance to continue living, an

opportunity worth taking given our lack of knowledge about her wishes and her medical condition. It turned out that she had already been struggling with complications of her diabetes. Her kidneys were failing, she had constant pain from her damaged peripheral nerves, and she had had many past hospitalizations for congestive heart failure. She felt discouraged about the direction her life was taking, though she had never talked with her physician about limiting medical intervention in any way (nor had her physician initiated the discussion). Over the next several days, when it became unequivocally clear that the patient was not going to regain consciousness, the life supports we initiated were discontinued and she died quietly. Though I had an uneasy feeling about our role in prolonging her suffering, I believe that, given our limited knowledge of her wishes and of her medical condition, aggressive medical treatment was both morally and medically correct. But I also wonder whether, if asked and fully informed, she would have wanted us to try such an invasive intervention, given her severe chronic illness and the poor likelihood of success. What were her goals for medical treatment, or her views about proper treatment when death was near? To my knowledge, these discussions never occurred, and we therefore assumed that she wanted every invasive medical measure to prolong her life.

The third cardiac arrest that I treated that day occurred on the surgical floor of the hospital. The patient was an eighty-year-old man who weighed 80 pounds. He was near death from widely metastatic lung cancer, yet was still receiving chemotherapy in a last-ditch effort to prolong his life. This unfortunate man was literally skin and bones, having lost 60 pounds from the ravages of advanced cancer. His surgeon had strongly recommended and carried out lung surgery in spite of clear evidence that the cancer was already widely spread, and he had continued chemotherapy despite its adverse effects and little evidence that it was helping. The surgeon adamantly believed that doctors and patients must always fight for life no matter what the burdens or the odds, and he had powerfully and repeatedly admonished his patient not to give up on medical treatment. As we ran into the room to begin cardiopulmonary resuscitation, we encountered a frail, wasted, dying elderly man. Could we possibly carry out this invasive, often brutal procedure? We didn't know the patient's wishes, but we did know that cardiopulmonary resuscitation is futile when patients are this severely ill. Every instinct in me said no to resuscitation—that our job for such a terminally ill person is to comfort and to ease the passage into death.

Unfortunately, the patient's attending surgeon also arrived, and his view was that the fight for this man's life must continue. In the hospital power hierarchy, the attending physician's decision clearly overrides that of the resident (and unfortunately sometimes that of the patient). Delaying cardiopulmonary resuscitation a few moments to clarify and negotiate would have ensured the patient's brain death. So we put a tube down this dying man's throat, and began pressing on his chest, shocking his heart, and giving him medicines. The bones in his chest were so frail that they fractured easily. His heart compressions were accompanied by a sickening crunch of broken ribs. There was no sign that he was responding in spite of repeated electrical shocks, chest compressions, and artificial ventilation, yet the surgeon still did not want to give up. After fifteen agonizing minutes, and no sustained response from the patient, the surgeon wondered out loud if he should surgically open the patient's chest so that he could directly massage the heart. I again told him my belief that further resuscitation was futile and that I was not going to participate anymore. After a difficult exchange in which my dedication to medicine was challenged, the resuscitation was stopped and the patient pronounced dead.

I left the room profoundly disturbed. I felt that not only had we violated this dying man, but I too had been violated by being forced to act in a way I found both personally and professionally intolerable. How could we repeatedly brutalize this poor man in the name of extending life? Could this possibly be what the Hippocratic Oath intended? Did this man know that he was dying, and if so, would he have chosen such an end? How could this attending surgeon, whom I knew from other settings to be a caring, competent individual, not see this man's suffering or the brutality and futility of the attempt at cardiopulmonary resuscitation? Should I have refused to participate from the start? Did I compromise myself and my professional future in the eyes of my superior by openly challenging his orders? The questions flowed fast and furiously. One answer emerged: When I left my residency and became an attending physician, I would do everything in my power to help patients make more informed choices toward the end of their lives, and to avoid futile, invasive medical interventions. I knew then, as I know now, that when someone is dying, alleviating suffering becomes more important than prolonging life.

I left the hospital that day excited about medicine's potential, but disturbed by its capacity to harm by blindly trying to extend life. If as physicians we have a mandate *always* to prolong life, then dying is an affront to our professional mission—something to be fought at all costs. The Hippocratic Oath that we take as physicians cannot be that simple.

MY GRANDPARENTS' DEATHS

My mother's father was a lucky man. At age seventy-nine, Poppy had never been ill enough to go to the hospital. He was a fiercely independent, hardworking first-generation Italian immigrant for whom illness and dependency would have been humiliating. As Poppy began to lose his health, he was terrified of his impending physical and mental deterioration, and the possibility of losing his independence. He told my mother that he wished that some morning in the near future he would simply not wake up. A few weeks later, before he had to give up the home he had built himself twenty years earlier, Poppy died one morning in his own bed, a broken glass on the floor the only sign of struggle.

At sixteen, this was my first personal contact with human death. Somehow I thought that death was for other families and that ours would live forever. His stillness at the wake, and the wrinkles on his unmoving hands, are images embedded in my memory. Why did he have to die? He had not been ill; he had not suffered. He was a good man who had not hurt anyone. Poppy's death saddened me terribly; but more profoundly, it began to shake my illusions of immortality. At least if he had been sick, or if he had been a "bad person," then perhaps such a sudden unanticipated death could be justified. It is remarkable how my experiences as a physician have turned these perceptions upside down.

My mother's mother died about twenty years earlier. I never knew her. My mother made a train trip to her deathbed when I was only a few weeks old so that my grandmother could see and hold me before she died. My grandmother had stomach cancer, and lost an extreme amount of weight before she died. The medical care that I am told she received makes me appreciate just how much progress we have made in the humane care of the dying. She was in severe pain for the last months of her life. Ordinarily a stoic woman, she was moaning in distress much of the time—unrelenting and unrelieved. Narcotics were used sparingly, and of course no one questioned the wisdom of the doctors in determining how much she needed. Part of that wisdom was not to tell my grandmother about her diagnosis. My grandfather and my uncle were the keepers of this secret that everybody knew, but nobody talked about.

Although by today's standards the medical care she received was lacking, she was fortunate in that her family provided loving care and support in her home. My aunt, the youngest of three children at age eighteen, left college to care for my grandmother throughout her unacknowledged illness. Forty years later, my aunt tearfully recalls sitting at my grandmother's bedside holding her hand, doing her best to comfort, but secretly wishing that her mother would die and escape the nightmare that she was living. The secrecy and shame surrounding the diagnosis isolated my grandmother from her family throughout her entire illness, and the physical pain she was forced to endure undermined any sense of well-being. Death must have come as a welcome relief.

My father's father was also unlucky. He died before I was born, having helplessly watched his eldest daughter die slowly from the relentless progression of a cancer in her throat. Even today, with all our sophisticated methods of pain relief and symptom management, such deaths from throat cancer are often anguishing. Three days before my aunt's welcome escape from this life, my grandfather dropped dead. The despair that he must have felt trying to comfort his daughter during her slow, painful demise presumably was more than he could bear. Our family lore suggests that my grandfather died of a "broken heart." Before I wrote my article about Diane, no one had told me the circumstances under which he died. To this day, my own father doesn't talk about it, though he is adamant about avoiding prolonged suffering in his own future. It is remarkable to me how many families have untold, secret, sometimes shame-filled stories about their helplessness in the face of extreme suffering at the end of loved ones' lives.

My father's mother died in her early nineties when I was in residency training (she would never tell us, and perhaps didn't know, exactly when she was born). Nana had come to this country from Ireland alone in her early twenties. She had worked hard her entire life, first simply to survive in a new country, and then to raise her family of four boys and two girls. She was a devout Catholic, and she worked as a cook for affluent families for much of her life. My father was the first of two sons to attend college, driven in large measure by my grandmother's values of hard work and intense independence.

Nana remained a dominant, fiercely independent force in our family until her last few years, when she developed coronary artery disease, congestive heart failure, and insidious, gradually progressive dementia. Unable explicitly to set limits on medical intervention—partly because of her dementia and partly because of her belief that God would take care of her through her physicians—Nana had implicitly given direction through statements like "I hope God will take me soon," or "Why do old people have to live so long?"

She began a series of trips to the local hospital for heart failure and fluid accumulation in her lungs, necessitating admission to the intensive-care unit and aggressive medical interventions like mechanical ventilation, central venous catheters, and tourniquets to control the fluids. She was too confused to understand the meaning of such bodily invasion, but fortunately her memory was short. However, the experience did stay with my father, who recalls sitting at Nana's bedside in the intensive-care unit with tubes coming out of every part of her body, despairing about the purpose of such inhumanity. If she could recover to a state that had meaning for her, then perhaps such invasiveness could be justified; but if not, it seemed closer to torture than humane care. As the heart failure and her dementia worsened, and hospitalization became more frequent, the reality that death was approaching became clearer. The possibility of shifting the goal of Nana's medical treatment away from extending life at all costs and toward lessening her suffering was never raised by her physicians.

Finally it became evident that she could no longer live alone. The family decided that Nana would live with my mother and father in another city. They did not ask my grandmother's doctor about the advisability of such a transfer for fear he would prohibit it because of the danger to her frail heart. Nana temporarily improved under my mother's loving care—she regained partial control of her bowels, became a little bit more alert, and was able to walk short distances with help. When I went home to visit, I found her in severe heart failure. We discussed some adjustments in her medicines that could be explored with her doctor, but it was clear to me that the end was near if she didn't improve.

A few weeks later, she suddenly slipped into a coma. It was a weekend, and her usual doctor was not available. The on-call doctor came for a house call at my parents' request. He examined Nana, and told my parents that there was no way she could survive without invasive medical interventions, and probably not even then. The doctor then told of his own father's death in a similar situation, and how he had been allowed to stay home to die in the presence of a loving family. Though my parents did not need much convincing about the preferability of keeping her home, their decision was reinforced and their potential guilt for not "doing everything" medically possible was allayed by this conversation. They agreed to "let nature take its course," and made up a bed in the den. My grandmother lay there, in the close attendance of a loving family, until she died peacefully twelve hours later. My parents feel that this substitute doctor gave them the most profound gift that a physician could give—assistance in achieving a dignified end to a very long and dignified life.

Just how significant this gift has been was brought home to my parents recently when one of their friends relayed the following story. Their friend's mother, who was dying of metastatic cancer, came to spend her final days with her children. They were able to provide loving, personal care over subsequent weeks, and their mother was able to make her own cremation arrangements and plan the kind of memorial service she wanted. She specifically did not want the ambulance or the police to be called when she died, since she feared being readmitted to the hospital. She subsequently drifted into a coma, and the family called the physician for reassurance and advice about how to proceed. They, too, got a substitute physician. Unfortunately, this physician not only would not do a house call, but also would not provide any advice other than calling an ambulance or the police.

The family was more anxious and uncertain after this conversation, but hung on at home because of the mother's explicit request, until they were sure she was dead. After dressing her in her favorite clothes, they finally called the police about how to proceed. The police called an ambulance, which rushed to the scene with lights and sirens. Though the patient had been dead for several hours, and had clearly stated her wishes to avoid medical intervention, the ambulance crew still tried cardiopulmonary resuscitation. When they determined that she was indeed dead and that resuscitation was futile, the police interrogated the family as if it were a homicide. After this unwanted, humiliating invasion there was still no death certificate, so the funeral director would not accept the body. The funeral home finally agreed to pick up the body, provided they could take it to the local hospital where the mother could be admitted to the Emergency Department and pronounced dead. The family will always bear the scars of this experience: complex feelings of guilt and shame about not having better protected their mother, and rage at the substitute doctor and the medical system that allowed their loving act to be turned inside out and trampled.

Thank God we had a doctor who allowed my grandmother the sanctity of a quiet, peaceful death at home.

LEARNING ABOUT DEATH IN MEDICAL SCHOOL

During my second year of training at the University of Rochester I was very lucky to take an elective on "Death and Dying" with Arthur Schmale, a senior physician on the staff who was trained in both internal medicine and psychiatry. As part of this elective, Dr. Schmale had us talk to patients who were near death about their hopes and fears. Unlike fully trained physicians, we were under no obligation to fight for life on behalf of these patients. Our obligation was to listen and learn, and perhaps to lessen some of the isolation that can accompany dying. This elective, taken by only a tiny fraction of our medical school class, was one of the rare moments in my training when death was openly acknowledged and explored as an inevitable part of medicine.

I learned from my conversations with these dying persons that their fears, hopes, and needs were not at all predictable by my own limited experience with death. Very few who understood their illness and its prognosis wanted to continue an all-out fight for life no matter what the personal consequences. Many knew that death was near, yet they had not lost hope. Hope, however, had often been redefined in terms of attending an important event in the near future, or resolving a troubling family conflict, or imagining that the next life would be more peaceful than the present. Their fears about death and dying were also unexpectedly individualized—ranging from abstract concerns about death itself to worries about unrelenting pain to fears about being left alone or about leaving their spouses or children.

Somehow we must train physicians to balance their drive to extend life with a mandate to listen to and learn from their patients, especially those who are dying. This delicate balance requires a much more judicious use of medical technology, combined with much more time spent informing and learning from patients themselves. Such exchanges are at the heart of humane medical care that serves patients who are ill, rather than treating disease and prolonging life as if the person does not exist.

Chapter 2

THE HIPPOCRATIC OATH AND THE CARE OF THE DYING

Reconsidering Medicine's Goals and Values

Physicians take the Hippocratic Oath upon completion of their medical degree. Two overriding directives of the oath are to prolong the lives of patients and to minimize their suffering. These deceptively simple, intuitively appealing principles often find themselves in conflict with one another in the treatment of the severely ill and the dying.

Modern medical treatment has a powerful potential to extend life, yet this same intervention sometimes unintentionally contributes to increased pain and suffering prior to death. Medicine's remarkable successes in treating some diseases have led many in our society to value the prolongation of life no matter what the personal consequences, while inadvertently minimizing the increase in human suffering that is often a byproduct. Rather than extending *meaningful* human life, as the Hippocratic Oath intends, medical interventions sometimes result in the prolongation of a painful death. The power and potential of medical technology to produce such diametrically opposed effects should be exercised with the utmost care and restraint.

The conflict between these two principles of the Hippocratic

Oath is relatively easy to resolve when treating a previously well person who has a potentially reversible illness. Asking patients temporarily to tolerate the seemingly unbearable distress that may be a byproduct of a disease and its treatment is usually justifiable when the chances for survival are good. If the patient lives, he or she is likely to return to a full life, presumably free of illness or persisting discomfort. In such circumstances, the value of saving a life overshadows what might otherwise be intolerable short-term suffering. We in medicine take great joy in using medicine's power creatively to help bring patients back from life-threatening illnesses, and to help them return to productive lives. Most patients who have survived such illnesses and treatments, even when agonizing and overwhelming at the time, are grateful and feel in retrospect that their ordeal was worthwhile. We also take pride in helping people adjust to chronic disease, and in using medical interventions to improve their function and enjoyment as well as prolong life.

On the other hand, the ability of medical intervention to extend the life of a dying person is very restricted. Even if such extension is possible, the desirability of doing so is highly dependent on the patient's view of quality of life, his or her desire to continue living, and the burdens of the medical treatment indicated. When treating a dying person, the balance within the Hippocratic Oath usually shifts. The discomfort that may be a byproduct of a specific life-prolonging medical treatment may not be acceptable. The primary goal usually shifts away from extending life toward lessening physical, emotional, and spiritual suffering. A corollary to this goal is to enhance a patient's control at a time when the options available are severely restricted.

Through my experiences in medical training, as well as those as a primary-care physician and a hospice consultant, I have come to believe that several fundamental values underlie care of the severely ill and dying. Some of these values are applicable to all aspects of the doctor-patient relationship, whereas others have particular importance to the care of the dying. These values appear to be relatively straightforward, yet many books and papers have been written exploring their derivation and implications. I try not to impose them upon my patients, but rather to express them openly and see if each patient's values and priorities differ from my own. The more my patients and I can reach agreement about what we are trying to achieve, the more we can use medicine's potential in a personalized way.

PERSONAL VALUES IN THE CARE OF THE DYING

1. *Informed, shared decision making:* Who could possibly argue that informed consent should be a fundamental tenet of medical care? Yet embedded in informed consent is a basic change in the power structure of medical care: the belief that the patient should be sharing more and more responsibility with the physician. I strongly believe that patients should take an active role in medical decision making, so that they learn as much as they can about the potential consequences of medical treatment or lack of treatment. Some of this is clearly self-protective. If a patient is unfortunate enough to experience an improbable adverse effect of treatment, he or she is less likely to hold me solely responsible, having been a fully informed participant. More fundamentally, however, if a treatment entails potential effects with far-reaching negative or positive consequences and considerable uncertainty, I feel that I have no right to make such decisions independently, except in emergencies when delay is dangerous or the patient is not capable of participating.

This is not to say that the patient should be deprived of the physician's advice and recommendations. Such "autonomy" would be a subtle form of abandonment, and absolutely should be avoided. Most patients need and want knowledgeable, experienced medical advice. But each physician must also realize his or her power to overly influence patients, especially when they are sick and vulnerable. The ideal informing process becomes one of shared learning. Patients learn about the medical facts, and the potential benefits and burdens of treatment, in the context of a realistic appraisal of their overall medical condition. Physicians, in turn, must learn of their patients' personal experiences and perceptions about the diagnosis, their current quality of life, and the amount of suffering they are willing to tolerate in the interest of potentially prolonging their life. Ideally, physician and patient make a decision by consensus at the end of these discussions, negotiating differences, but respecting the fact that the patient will ultimately experience the benefits and/or the burdens of treatment.

There are many reasons why such fully informed decision making often does not occur. A patient may be too sick or too cognitively impaired to participate, and sometimes medical decisions have to be made too rapidly for shared decision making. Some patients, for varied and complex reasons, don't want to be full participants, preferring to leave the decisions in the benevolent hands of their physicians. It is also very difficult for doctors and patients to discuss information about odds and risks and develop a shared understanding; for example, even experienced physicians will assign widely different probability numbers to such words as "likely" and "improbable." Furthermore, if a treatment has a 40 percent chance of curing an illness and a 60 percent chance of producing death, some individuals will make different choices depending on whether the same statistical information is presented in terms of the likelihood of living as opposed to the likelihood of dying. Despite these and other pitfalls, informed, shared decision making remains an ideal to be pursued.

2. *Person-centered care:* I have now been practicing medicine for twelve years, and I find that the doctor-patient relationship becomes more rewarding as I get to know my patients better and better. I envision my professional task as helping my patients use medical interventions in a highly individualized fashion. Caring for and working with my patients through sickness and health, through hard times and good times, creates an increasing sense of trust and connection. This can then provide a foundation for facing tragedy when and if it arises.

I appreciated and respected Diane's tenacity and independence as she came to grips with problems related to alcoholism and depression over a period of ten years. I knew that Diane would approach the diagnosis of leukemia by taking charge in her own way. My job was to give her the medical information she needed to make informed decisions, and to help her explore the personal and medical consequences of the options she was considering. The medical care for acute leukemia in every medical textbook includes chemotherapy as well as treatment of predictable side effects and complications. The person-centered approach to Diane's leukemia started with my taking a large step back at her insistence—being forced in fact to think openly and critically with her about whether or not even to initiate chemotherapy.

There are at least two persons in any person-centered approach. The physician, far from being a passive vehicle for the patient's wishes, is instead an active participant whose knowledge, beliefs, and experience are vital to informed decisions. Thinking through the true burdens of leukemia treatment and the odds of success from Diane's perspective helped me eventually to accept her decision to forgo treatment. But I did not do so without a fight. I clearly let her know my wish that she consent to chemotherapy, and my concerns about her refusal. Part of me wanted to falsely color her decision by minimizing the toxicity of leukemia chemotherapy, but she was too inquisitive and our relationship was too honest for that; besides, she reminded me firmly that it was she, not I, who would be experiencing chemotherapy. Diane had thought extensively about severe illness and the possibility of death in the past, and her decision was consistent with deeply held values.

Person-centered care has two fundamental implications. First is the individually tailored application of medical care to each person, guided by the patient's wishes and goals for treatment. Second, the physician combines medical expertise with knowledge and caring about her patient as a person to keep her deeply invested in the outcome of the treatment. The patient ultimately controls the decisions made, but under the guidance of an actively involved, medically knowledgeable physician.

3. Power and limitations of medical care: I have a strong love and a deep respect for the power of medicine. Infections like pneumococcal pneumonia and cancers like Hodgkin's lymphoma that were highly lethal only a few decades ago are now curable. Few experiences are more gratifying than using medical technology to help a gravely ill patient through the dark stages of a life-threatening illness to full recovery and independence. Also eminently satisfying is the use of medical interventions to help a chronically ill person function and feel better.

But there are limits to medical intervention. Most treatments, no matter how well intended, have the potential to do harm as well as good. Particularly when patients are nearing the end of life, or when their illness entails considerable suffering, all potential outcomes of each medical intervention require careful examination. Physicians are generally sophisticated at weighing the medical benefits and burdens in terms of treating diseases and prolonging life, but less able to include the personal side of these considerations. Earlier, I described examples where the invasiveness and brutality of cardiopulmonary resuscitation were clearly justifiable for one patient with an acute heart attack, but not for another patient with end-stage lung cancer. Since the probability and the significance of success differed drastically in these two circumstances, it is very likely that most informed patients would make different decisions faced with these two situations.

I believe that most physicians tend to understate the potential adverse consequences of medical interventions in their discussions with patients and their families. We also tend to minimize the severity of a patient's illness and to put the best face on their prognosis, so that the context for making informed decisions is often lacking. Patients, like physicians, want medicine to be more powerful than it usually is. They often wish to be less sick than they really are and will silently collude with their doctors by not asking direct questions about prognosis. If this collusion were benign, perhaps it could be justified in the interest of softening a harsh reality. Sadly, avoiding discussions and decisions about death too frequently has profound negative consequences.

4. *Medicalization of death:* With the geographic dispersion of the extended family, medicine and technology have taken an increasing role in providing meaning and ritual at the end of people's lives. In some circumstances, medicine has almost become a religion, and prolonging life at all costs by using medical technology is its primary objective. The intensive-care units have become the end-of-life shrines, and cardiopulmonary resuscitation the final ceremony. In this religion, death is fought off no matter what the personal or economic costs. Dying patients can be tied down and fed with nasogastric feeding tubes so that they won't starve, and the Supreme Court can allow a state's interest in the "sanctity of life" to overrule the request of caring families to discontinue the feeding tube of an irreversibly brain-damaged person who has previously said she would not want to be "kept alive as a vegetable."

In medical training and practice, the prolongation of life is given a much higher value than the lessening of human suffering, even in the care of the dying. Eighty percent of deaths in the

United States occur today in hospitals and chronic-care facilities. A walk down the corridors of our hospitals and nursing homes can be sobering. Tube feeding to ensure nutritional balance has replaced personal feeding with its sense of human contact, touch, and taste. Physically restraining patients with vests and belts to keep them from falling has replaced the caring supervision of families or contact with staffs, whose primary job has become monitoring medical technology rather than caring for patients as people. Despite increasing salaries and benefits, it is increasingly difficult to find nurses and physicians who want to provide direct personal care for patients.

An inadvertent and unintended side effect of medicine's growing effectiveness is that the dying process has been elongated. For those whose quality of life remains high or even satisfactory, this can be a good outcome. But for those who are suffering greatly and those who lose the mental capacity to refuse treatment, it has become harder and harder to die. Now almost no one dies directly from cancer, and the infections that used to be the "old man's friend" are reflexively treated with potent antibiotics. Through transfusions, antibiotics, and artificial feeding, dying can be unthinkingly extended well beyond the point where living has any meaning to either the individual or the family. These well-intended treatments are often continued without careful analysis until the suffering that they are unintentionally contributing to is undeniable to all concerned. Only when outward suffering has become overwhelming and unbearable does an acceptance of the inevitability of death change the direction of care so that comfort is emphasized over prolonging life.

There are some signs of positive change. Living Wills and Health Care Proxies (see Chapter 10) are now legally recognized entities that can guide future treatment should one lose the mental capacity to participate in medical decisions oneself. Many patients are also being offered the option of forgoing cardiopulmonary resuscitation in the hospital, particularly if they are severely ill.

"Comfort care," as exemplified in hospice care, is an alternative being presented to some terminally ill patients. Comfort care emphasizes care of the person and his/her suffering, with lesser attention to the disease and the extension of life. Comfort care puts a higher value on relieving symptoms, human contact, and care of the person than on treatment of the underlying disease. Comfort care answers many of the criticisms that I have described about the care of the dying, and in my opinion it is offered to far too few patients much too late in the dying process. There are also tragic circumstances where even competently applied comfort care still cannot ensure a dignified, acceptable death.

5. *The care of the dying:* The patient's quest for a dignified death should be a fundamental part of the equation for end-of-life medical decisions. This highly personal endeavor has been explored and exalted in great literature and art, yet it is curiously minimized or even ignored by the profession of medicine. Perhaps it could help medical practitioners discover more meaning and direction in the care of their dying patients than they currently find in the unthinking (and unfeeling) application of life-prolonging medical technology.

Many of my most touching experiences in the practice of medicine have been working with dying patients and their families to somehow face and solve the tragic predicaments that dying can present. The decision to use comfort care defines the goal of the treatment, but the exact form it takes will be highly idiosyncratic—depending on the disease, the individual, the family, and the social environment.

As the former medical director of a community-based hospice program, and in my own general practice, I sometimes found myself talking to a neurosurgeon about new techniques for deadening a nerve that was producing an overwhelming amount of pain in a patient with metastatic cancer who otherwise had an excellent quality of life. I might next have an intense conversation with a dialysis patient about whether to discontinue treatment, making sure that he understands the consequences of such a decision, that his thinking is not distorted by depression, and that I fully understand the reasons he is raising the question at this time.

I have marveled at the courage some patients have shown in accepting death, whereas others have used that same energy to vigorously fight off death until the end. My role has been to inform and learn from each person; to help them make the best choices, given their values and the nature of their illnesses; to ensure that they did not feel unnecessarily isolated; and to try to give them as much control and latitude as possible.

Caring humanely for the dying and trying to help them find a dignified death is a fundamentally vital role for physicians. It has little of the surface appeal of life-saving medical technology, and it is certainly not reimbursed at a fraction of the rate of an invasive medical procedure. Yet if judicious use of medicine's potential is central to our mission as physicians, then its personal and professional rewards are unparalleled.

M A R K

Mark was the kind of son any one of us would love to have. He was eighteen years old, bright, friendly, athletic, and headed for college. He was an only child, and his mother had devoted much of her adult life to ensuring his emotional and physical well-being. His parents were divorced, but they continued to find common ground in their love, concern, and devotion to their son.

Mark had one of those eighteen-year-old bodies that leave us all envious: sleek, muscular, filled with possibility and assurance that life would last forever. Unfortunately, Mark's heart did not match his body. It began to deteriorate without warning from a progressive condition that defied diagnosis and was largely untreatable. Not only was his heart failing as a pump, but it was prone to dangerous, life-threatening arrhythmias that required more and more time in the hospital. During one of these hospitalizations, he had several cardiac arrests. He was successfully revived with cardiopulmonary resuscitation, but emerged from the experience with a small stroke that limited his ability to do calculations and to process certain kinds of abstract facts.

It was at this point that I first came to know Mark. As he was struggling to make sense of what had happened to him and to understand what his future now held, he was losing faith in his physicians and in the medical system. He wanted desperately to continue a normal life—including athletics, parties, alcohol, and college. Yet he faced the need for potentially toxic medications, dietary and activity restrictions, and the possibility of an experimental pacemaker that could sense a rhythm disturbance and shock his heart automatically. His long-term outlook for survival was limited without a heart transplant.

Mark hated to talk about his illness. Left alone, it was clear that his youthful instincts would have told him to forget all these prescriptions and proscriptions, and to continue living life to the fullest. Yet because of the dangers of his heart condition, Mark had to face up to the potential consequences of each of the courses open to him. If he stopped everything and tried to return completely to his normal life, he would likely have another cardiac arrest and die or suffer severe residual neurological problems. If he took the medications and restricted his activities, the odds of this happening would be considerably less. If he took the medications, restricted his activity, and allowed us to surgically implant a permanent pacemaker that could automatically "restart" his heart should it stop, his odds of fatal or disabling cardiac arrest would be even less, but there were still no guarantees. Finally, we explored the complex possibility of a heart transplant, balancing its invasiveness and the immediate risks of the *surgery and immune-suppressing treatment against the improved odds of long-term survival.*

After a series of conversations, it was clear that Mark and his parents understood the options, including our recommendation that he take medications and have the special pacemaker inserted. Although Mark avoided thinking about being ill, it was evident that he was thinking deeply about his choices. Unlike most eighteen-year-olds, Mark had to face the possibility of death. He also had very strong feelings about how he wanted to live, and how far he was willing to compromise in order to lessen his risk. He agreed to take the medication, to restrict his most strenuous activity, to curtail alcohol, but not to have the pacemaker. In his eyes, the pacemaker would unequivocally alter his self-image, identifying him permanently and visibly as a sick person. For him, this was too high a price. He also did not want to consider a heart transplant at this time when he could still be quite active, but did not completely rule it out in the future. He made it abundantly clear that if he had a cardiac arrest and emerged from it with significant brain damage, he would not want to be kept alive. He wanted to live as fully as possible, but had tremendous fear about being forced to live in a severely compromised, restricted way.

Mark had been his mother's heart and soul. It was hard for her to allow him to go to college, to become independent, and to begin to make his own way. Yet she had managed to let go, and had begun to re-explore her own independence, a move that she saw as important for both Mark and herself. With Mark's illness, her protective mothering instincts resurfaced with a vengeance. She wanted to take Mark back under her wing, to protect him and guide him through the dangers he faced, as she had done so successfully when he was a little boy. She wanted him to return home, restrict his activities, and to follow all the medical recommendations to the letter. She was profoundly afraid of losing him. Mark and his mother had several conversations about what returning home would mean and how important it was for him to maintain some semblance of a life he deemed worth living. After considerable soul-searching, Mark's mother was finally (albeit reluctantly) able to allow him to return to school.

With his medications stabilized, Mark did return to school. Though he had difficulty academically because of the residual effects of his stroke, he lived fully and independently. He told us later of the joys of white-water rafting and skiing, and of the many new friends he made. He had two hospitalizations for adjustments in his anti-arrhythmic medication, but no major complications. Outwardly he looked robust, the picture of health and omnipotence. Yet inside the deceptive shell lay a critically ill heart, and the potential for sudden death at any moment.

Mark lived largely on his own terms for a year and a half. Ironically, his cardiac arrest occurred when he was home visiting his mother. Mark's mother found him unconscious on the floor and immediately started cardiopulmonary resuscitation. She lived out her worst nightmare, frantically trying to revive her son while awaiting the ambulance. Through her skillful efforts, Mark's heart began beating again. He was transported to the hospital and admitted to the coronary care unit. We were able to stabilize his heart rhythm, but his brain was severely damaged. After several days, his brain showed no sign of recovery. The electroencephalogram showed minimal, grossly abnormal activity, though it did not meet the criteria for complete brain death. Mark's brain was not going to recover, though we could conceivably keep him alive for a long time with the use of invasive life supports.

Mark's parents (and I) were devastated by what had happened. Though Mark's mother had probably saved his life, she agonized about how she had performed cardiopulmonary resuscitation, and whether if she had arrived home earlier, things would have been different. We also second-guessed the decisions we had made with Mark that allowed for less than the most aggressive and restrictive of interventions. As we reanalyzed the decisions, it was clear that Mark made his own decisions with a full understanding of the possibilities.

After extensive self-examination and the beginning of grief, Mark's family and I had to come to grips with what to do next. Faced squarely, each of us knew that Mark would not want to be kept alive in this fashion—if his brain was not going to recover, then he would rather be dead. Yet how can you ask a mother and father to let go of their only child, their pride and joy, the embodiment of much of their future aspirations and hopes? Their courage in facing this tragic moment will always be a source of inspiration to me. They were able to put themselves in Mark's place, and to transcend their own anguish to look at the decision based on what he had told us. From that perspective, it was clear: Mark would want us to stop everything and let him die in the manner in which he had wished to live—independent and unencumbered by medical technology.

When a young person dies like this in the hospital, it can bring out the best or the worst in the system. In Mark's case, it brought out the best. The nurses, the residents, the doctors, and the family all understood who this young man had been and what he had wanted. We each supported one another as plans were made to take him off the respirator and to discontinue the life-sustaining medications. Those who wanted to were able to say goodbye to Mark in their own way. When the time came, one of the nurses and I disconnected the respirator in the presence of his mother and father. Mark died several minutes later, a guitar pick in his hand as a symbol of who he had been and what might have been.

Those of us who are parents were especially shaken by this experience. It is hard enough to contemplate our own mortality, but to face the possible deaths of our children is ordinarily out of reach. Yet the courage that Mark's parents showed in letting him be who he was, and then in letting go rather than forcing him to be who he wasn't, was exceptional. Mark, too, helped us by being clear in advance about what he wanted and didn't want. Armed with a clear vision of his wishes, the process of letting him go had a clarity that is so often missing. Since Mark had let us know in no uncertain terms that he would rather be dead than alive in a helpless, dependent state, our obligation to him was clear. Though each of us had to contend with our grief about his death, and the possibility of our own children's deaths, that grief was not compounded by uncertainty about whether we did what Mark would have wanted at the end.

Chapter 3

DEATH OR CHI-CHI?

The Burdens of Aggressive Medical Treatment

A frightening, very dark parable has passed through the halls of many medical centers. It captures a disturbing, torturous process that can contaminate the medical care of dying patients. The actual metaphor may vary, but the invasive treatment described, with its deep loss of meaning for all concerned, rings true to health-care providers who are on the front lines providing medical care in the United States today. The parable goes as follows:

Three sailors are shipwrecked on a remote island, and captured by a primitive tribe. They are tied up by the tribesmen and brought before a tribunal of elders. The elders gave the first sailor a choice: "What would you rather have, death or Chi-Chi?" The sailor hesitated only a moment. "I know what death is, and I surely don't want it. I will take Chi-Chi." The sailor was then slowly skinned alive by the tribesmen, and had his heart cut out while he was still conscious, after which he died.

After watching this horrible ritual, the second sailor was brought before the tribunal. He was much more circumspect, and thought very carefully before giving his answer. "I certainly don't want to die, but I also don't want to be tortured and die anyway. But maybe Chi-Chi changes. Maybe it's a relative phenomenon. Maybe it won't happen to me. Given these limited choices, I guess I will take Chi-Chi." The second sailor was then subjected to the same ordeal, skinned alive, after which his heart was cut out while it was still beating.

The third sailor was then offered the same choice. His perspective was radically altered by the disturbing ritual he has witnessed. "Maybe death isn't all that bad. I certainly don't want Chi-Chi. I guess I will take death." The elders looked a bit surprised, and said, "Okay, but first Chi-Chi."

I have told this chilling tale in a variety of lectures and workshops about end-of-life decision making. Health-care workers, particularly those who are the medical "tribesmen," are stimulated by it and find disturbing aspects of their work acknowledged by the story. Our "tribesmen," of course, are the nurses, physicians' assistants, nurse practitioners, residents, and medical students who must carry out the orders generated by the "elders" who represent the attending doctors. Unfortunately, sometimes the tribesmen carrying out the medical treatments and the elders making the decisions are very different people, aware of vastly different aspects of the patient's experience. The elders may be unaware of the personal burdens of the medical treatment, and the tribesmen may be unaware of its underlying purpose and goals. When the possibility for meaningful recovery becomes remote, then burdensome treatment begins to feel more like torture than a difficult means to a higher purpose. If the decision makers successfully shield themselves from the true burdens of treatment or from the reality that a patient is dying, then medical treatment can unintentionally prolong and dehumanize the dying process. Those providing hands-on continuous care have more difficulty denying patient suffering and the reality of impending death, so our medical tribesmen often feel torn between carrying out the chief's orders and participating in a demoralizing process that feels very much like Chi-Chi.

Traditional medical treatments, of course, also have the potential to save lives. Saving a life and contributing to a torturous death are awesome and diametrically opposed possible outcomes. The case of the elderly man near death from incurable lung cancer, who still received chemotherapy and prolonged cardiopulmonary resuscitation, was an example of a dehumanizing form of Chi-Chi. From my perspective as a resident, I was brutalizing this man with an invasive medical intervention that had no hope of working. I felt that we were simply placating his attending physician, who believed that, no matter what the costs or consequences, we should fight for life to the bitter end. The patient's wishes are not relevant if medicine's mission is always first and foremost to fight for life. The odds of cardiopulmonary resuscitation prolonging this man's life were infinitesimal. Even if successful, the amount of time gained would be hours, days, or at most a few weeks before his unrelenting cancer would have led to the failure of another part of his body.

If this patient shared his doctor's wish to fight against death no matter what the consequences or the odds, then at least we as medical "tribesmen" could hang on to the belief that we were granting a dying person his very difficult last wish. Uninformed, however, the patient became the victim of a brutal medical death ritual. The effect upon health-care providers who have to inflict such torture without being apprised of its purpose or of the patient's personal goals is devastating and demoralizing. The blind fight for life without regard to the specific individual undermines the fundamental values of the profession. It can become a perversion of the Hippocratic Oath, which requires that the fight for life be balanced by careful attention to the alleviation of human suffering. I believe that this imbalance of medical values partially explains the migration away from patient-care careers in medicine and nursing at a time when medical intervention has never been more effective.

Yet many times the outcome of invasive medical treatment is uncertain. Survival is a long shot, with poor odds, but not impossible. To get there, one may have to endure days, weeks, or even months of Chi-Chi. Difficult decisions about whether to use invasive medical treatments are faced every day by doctors, and more and more they are being openly shared with patients and their families. They are extraordinarily hard to grasp, particularly when death must be compared with a slim chance at life—a chance that may entail considerable discomfort, perhaps bordering on torture, as part of the treatment. Although death is virtually certain if one forgoes aggressive medical treatment, many times patients will live for considerable periods of time before it comes. Stopping invasive treatment opens the potential of keeping the patient relatively comfortable for the time that remains, using the techniques of comfort care. Comfort care's goal is to treat patients' suffering more than their disease, and to enhance human contact more than medical intervention. Unfortunately, comfort care is often offered very late, if at all, to most severely ill patients.

My acceptance of Diane's refusal to undergo medical treatment for her leukemia was one of the more controversial aspects of the article I wrote about our joint decision making. After all, it has been said, she had a 25 percent chance of life! That's a lot better than "nothing" (i.e., death), and a lot better than the odds of many other treatments that we ordinarily do. I too had a difficult time accepting this aspect of Diane's decision. She had fought and overcome serious, complex problems with alcoholism, vaginal cancer, and depression in the past. I hoped that her initial refusal could be overcome through careful consideration of the options and their consequences, once the shock of the diagnosis wore off. In the course of my subsequent conversations with Diane and others, I tried to take a cold, objective look at the requirements of acute leukemia treatment, and then to fathom what this treatment would mean to Diane.

Both the medical "elders" and the "tribesmen" have intense, mixed feelings of dread, anticipation, fear, and excitement when a new patient with acute leukemia is admitted to the hospital. The treatment is relentless, including several courses of chemotherapy, followed by whole-body radiation, and then bone-marrow transplantation. Each stage of treatment is harsh, with predictable, severe complications of infection, anemia, and bleeding. Each phase requires long periods of hospitalization during which one becomes extraordinarily sick and dependent on a large medical staff with varying levels of caring and competence. Seventy-five percent of patients die before treatment is completed, 25 percent in each of the three phases. The treatment process could aptly be equated in the worst of times with Chi-Chi, but if you are in the 25 percent who survive, you have a chance at a long life free of ✓ disease. Many survivors find that the painful fight they endured can be justified by the extraordinary result of a return to a full and productive life. Of course one would choose life, no matter what the costs. The treatment of acute leukemia is one of the successes about which we in medicine are most proud. It is a clear example of the triumph of medical technology over a previously fatal condition.

But what of the 75 percent of patients who don't survive? Unfortunately, they too undergo Chi-Chi. In retrospect, their families often have much more negative feelings about treatment, and about the amount of advance information they were given. In correspondence emanating from my article about Diane, many family members of leukemia patients who did not survive lamented the torture that their relatives went through before death, and wondered about the value of such a cruel and invasive process. The four previous acute leukemia patients at our hospital died very difficult deaths in varying stages of treatment. We hoped that Diane's odds would be better given these bad outcomes—that the odds would now favor a patient of ours surviving.

Diane had a strong intuition that she would be one of the 75 percent who did not survive. She was also very proud and independent, both physically and emotionally, and knew that she would find the treatment process in the hospital overwhelming and degrading. In the past, she did not even like to visit a doctor, much less to be immersed in the medical system and dependent on physicians, nurses, health aides, and technological intervention. Furthermore, the one in four chances of surviving were overshadowed for her by the three in four chances of dying—and being medically invaded along the way. In pressing her to change her mind, I wanted her to understand that refusing treatment did not guarantee a comfortable death. In fact, she would be subject to some of the same complications. Though together we would try to manage these problems at home, and her dignity and choice would be respected in each decision, there were no guarantees of an easy death given her severe disease. A comfort-oriented approach, however, would clearly take the treatment in a drastically different direction, driven by the goal of minimizing suffering and maximizing personal control rather than using all means necessary to prolong her life.

For Diane, the choice was clear: to spend the time she had left at home with her family, living each day as fully as she could. She was enrolled in a hospice program at home. This meant that a team of caregivers who were experienced in comfort care shared their expertise to ensure that her suffering was minimized and her choices were respected and adhered to. It also meant that skilled nurses, health aides, social workers, and clergy were available to assist her in her home, depending on her needs and wishes. Surprisingly, she lived for three months without being hospitalized (other than three brief visits to the inpatient hospice for transfusions)—time that she made the most of with her family and closest friends. The time was not easy, nor was it devoid of physical and existential suffering. But for Diane it had meaning, dignity, and control, and was consistent with her personal values. Even though her decision to forgo medical treatment made us uncomfortable, her outcome compared favorably with the extreme physical suffering and anguish experienced by our four previous leukemia patients, each of whom died in the midst of excruciating battles between medical technology, acute leukemia, and death.

It has been argued that it was disappointing, and even morally wrong, for Diane to have given up without a fight or without "suffering enough." I find these arguments sanctimonious, naive, and disturbing. To begin with, to say that Diane did not struggle with and fully explore the frightening choices she faced is both presumptuous and wrong. Secondly, when one takes a careful look at these options from the perspective of the person who must endure all the consequences, choosing treatment for acute leukemia is not a foregone conclusion. Diane helped me to view this decision more objectively, and would repeatedly remind her family and me that it was she who would be going through the process. When faced with the choice between a relatively controlled and dignified death, and very invasive medical treatment that had a 75 percent chance of resulting in death anyway, she chose the former, which was more acceptable to her.

A third criticism has been that Diane "took the easy way out." Those who make this argument argue that suffering prior to death is part of the human condition, and that to minimize or foreshorten it is immoral, or at least demonstrates a weakness in character. This harsh, puritanical approach to fighting death pervades current medical thinking, and Western culture in general. It maximizes the potential of medical treatment to prolong dying, and to have death be dominated by technology. Imposing medical intervention prior to death upon those who have other values, or wish to make different choices, is unacceptable. Going "gentle into that good night" with one's dignity and sense of self intact is certainly as morally acceptable as raging "against the dying of the light."

Yet these philosophies have radically different implications for medical care. There is nothing easy about accepting the inevitability of death—Diane experienced more than her share of anguish in coming to accept her condition and its implications. Our obligation in medicine is to understand and explore, not to judge or impose.

THE LONG ROAD HOME

We saw an earlier example of a dying patient being victimized by his physician's need to fight for life to the bitter end. In contrast, Diane took charge in a highly uncertain, volatile medical situation by going against medical norms and initial advice, and choosing a comfort-oriented approach where suffering was minimized but eventual death was certain. Another common dynamic is when a chronically ill patient develops a severe illness that has the possibility of being reversible, but more probably will result in death despite invasive medical treatment. Such patients may even have given advance directives stating their wish for comfort measures if medical treatment is futile, but these directives don't cover circumstances where the odds of surviving an arduous medical course are very small. In such circumstances, medical treatment is not futile; but the added personal suffering that is a burden of treatment is disturbing, given the poor odds of survival.

M R. H.

I had known Mr. H. for eight years. He had many medical problems, including diabetes mellitus, severe arthritis, vascular disease, and hypertension. He had survived complicated and potentially dangerous surgeries—among them joint replacements and an abdominal aneurysm repair. In spite of the risks of these interventions, he pulled through with relative ease. Though he knew his luck couldn't hold out forever, he remained optimistic and independent. When we discussed future use of cardiopulmonary resuscitation, he was not ready to decide. "You decide," he would say. "You will know what is best when the time comes." Though I challenged him to share that responsibility with me, he was not ready to make a binding decision. He did say that if we initiated invasive treatment and it looked like he would not recover fully or regain his independence, then he would definitely want it discontinued.

Mr. H. asked his niece, with whom he lived and had a very close relationship, to make decisions on his behalf should he lose the ability to make them on his own (i.e., she would be his Health Care Proxy). At age seventy-eight, with several chronic medical conditions, he knew that death was not too far away, but he also wanted desperately to keep living, provided he could remain of sound mind and independent body. He had no desire whatsoever to live in a nursing home, to be overly dependent on his family, or to lose his cognitive abilities. He made it clear that he would rather be dead than in such a state. He did not particularly like to discuss these issues and clearly would have preferred for me to decide his medical matters on my own. Though I generally resist taking sole responsibility for such decisions, I felt that I understood Mr. H.'s wishes well enough to proceed.

The end of Mr. H.'s life did not come easily. He had a heart attack and was admitted to the hospital. After an initial period of stabilization, his lungs became congested, and he needed to be intubated (have a breathing tube put down his throat into his lungs) and put on a mechanical ventilator (a breathing machine). While on the ventilator, he began hallucinating and became very frightened. He felt he was being assaulted, and couldn't even recognize close family members. He required large amounts of sedatives to keep him from fighting the breathing machine and the staff, and to allow him to escape his nightmare. Over subsequent days it was evident that not only was there fluid in his lungs from the heart attack, but he also had pneumonia. These were all reversible complications, but their treatment required at least an additional week of heavy sedation on the breathing machine, along with intravenous antibiotics and other treatments.

Mr. H.'s niece (acting as his Health Care Proxy) and I explored the medical options. She hated to see him in a state of physical and emotional chaos, and thought that perhaps we should stop treatment from the outset and let him die in peace. In her eyes he was dying, and further treatment seemed more like torture than compassionate care. I, on the other hand, saw his acute problems as potentially reversible, and felt that his odds of a full recovery were still significant enough to proceed. We tried to figure out what he would want us to do, and agreed to continue current treatments but not to do further cardiopulmonary resuscitation should his heart stop. We also agreed that if he developed another major complication, we would switch our attention entirely to keeping him comfortable, stopping all life-prolonging treatments, and letting him die in peace.

After two weeks of extreme suffering but no major medical deterioration, Mr. H. was eventually taken off the breathing machine. His lungs had cleared of pneumonia and fluid, and his heart had stabilized from the heart attack. He was initially quite confused, and fortunately had little memory of the preceding two weeks. His mental alertness gradually returned to normal, and we began to work on his walking and independence. When we discussed his recollection of the past few weeks, he described being jailed and assaulted. In spite of our reassurance, he remained uncertain about how much of his nightmare really happened. He was simultaneously appreciative and very wary of the staff. He was now completely certain that he would never want such treatment again, even if death was the alternative. His spirit and fight had been broken, and he felt that he might be better off in a nursing home—a thought that would have been anathema to him in past conversations.

We worked hard with Mr. H. to help him rediscover his will to live. Though we agreed not to use heroic measures to prolong his life should he become severely ill again, we also eventually agreed that working to regain his physical independence was better than his giving up completely and staying in bed all the time. His confidence began to return, and he began first to eat and then to walk independently. Realistic hopes of going home surfaced. Perhaps the ordeal had been worth it.

Unfortunately, Mr. H.'s medical condition did not stabilize. He started to complain of pain in his right foot when walking. Shortly thereafter his toes became blackened. The blood supply to his leg had failed, and severely painful gangrene began to inch slowly up his leg. We tried to control the pain with continuous around-the-clock morphine, but Mr. H. hated the sedation and confusion that accompanied this treatment when the dose was high enough to relieve his pain. Our goal was to keep him comfortable, but standard treatment with narcotic pain relievers was not proving effective, so we explored other alternatives with him. One of the options was amputation above his knee where the circulation was adequate. Because the pain was unrelenting with no clear end in sight, and because he didn't like the side effects of the pain medicines, Mr. H., his niece, and I finally selected the amputation. As is often the case when illness reaches this phase, none of the choices was a good one. Mr. H. knew the risk of surgery was high, given his recent heart attack, and that there would likely be some postoperative pain, but he thought these risks worth the potential of being free from the severe, unrelenting pain of gangrene. We also reaffirmed our agreement that no invasive measures would be used to prolong his life. Our purpose in choosing the surgery was not to prolong his life (he was in fact now very ready to die), but rather to keep him more comfortable for the time he had left.

The surgery went without a hitch. He was back in his room, free of pain, optimistic, and chatting within two hours. Given his severe arthritis and the overall prognosis, Mr. H. decided that he didn't want to fight the battle of learning how to use a prosthesis (an artificial limb). He began to talk more and more about dying. Though he was not in a hospice, a comfort-oriented philosophy now governed his care in the hospital. Reluctantly he acquiesced to exploring the options as to where he could live his remaining days, given his physical needs. Inpatient hospice and other nursing facilities where comfort care is offered were explored with Mr. H. and his niece.

After a brief calm, during which he was pain-free and began to achieve some peace about his condition, Mr. H. suddenly developed chest pain and shortness of breath. His blood pressure dropped. He was having another heart attack. This time we treated his heart pain and shortness of breath with morphine, but, as we had agreed, we did not transfer him to the coronary care unit and did not use invasive life-sustaining measures. We did give him fluids to try to bring his blood pressure back up, and a potent narcotic to relieve his pain, but his kidneys stopped working, his heart was failing, and death was imminent. With consciousness already compromised by his low blood pressure, the sedation that came with the morphine was now a welcome side effect. He lived another thirty-six hours on the edge of death, in and out of consciousness from constant sedation and low blood pressure, with his family in attendance. His death was a relief to us all. It had indeed been a long, unintentionally harsh road for Mr. H., a road none of us had intended nor would have wished for a man whom we deeply respected and cared about.

I have struggled and reexamined my decisions in Mr. H.'s care, and the countless other patients I have cared for who experienced Chi-Chi on the road to death. There is no question in retrospect *from Mr. H.'s, his family's, or my perspective that he would have been better off had we let him die with comfort and dignity during his initial admission to the coronary care unit. Could we have seen the future, then his experience of Chi-Chi could have been prevented or at least minimized. Yet we as physicians are certainly not omniscient, and without clear evidence either that Mr. H. would not survive in a manner he would find acceptable or that he did not want to undergo treatments with such severe burdens, I feel even in retrospect that we were compelled to proceed.*

The decision to continue aggressive medical intervention, especially under those circumstances where the odds of harm are high, needs to be constantly reexamined. When a patient decides that the suffering which occurs is too much to bear, or when the odds of full recovery become too remote, then the goal of treatment may need to be shifted away from prolonging life toward promoting comfort and lessening suffering. As Mr. H.'s course illustrates, even when a less medically aggressive approach is chosen, there remain difficult trade-offs between pain and sedation, and choices about major interventions that, though well intended, may have undesirable outcomes.

The variations on these complex end-of-life decisions are endless, and defy simple solutions or rules. The 20 percent of the health-care dollar currently being spent on the last two months of life attests not only to the social and economic costs of our fight against death, but also to the degree to which we use expensive medical technology to try to intervene in the terminal phases of an illness. The suffering that patients like Mr. H. go through speaks to the disturbing personal costs of such battles. Put in statistical terms, Mr. H. probably had a 10 percent chance of surviving fully, and perhaps another 20 percent chance of surviving but enduring a major, permanently disabling complication in the process that would keep him from returning to an independent life. Translated into individual terms, that means that out of every ten patients who enter the hospital in such a condition, seven will die at some time in this long process of medical treatment. Two out of the ten will survive, but have a major disabling complication that prohibits their returning to independent life. Finally, one out of the ten will survive and eventually be able to return to his or her former life. Clearly, such varied outcomes and poor odds mean that patients need to be informed if possible before embarking on such treatment odysseys. Putting patients through medical intervention when the odds of meaningful survival are so low and the odds of severe suffering so high requires as much informed consent as is possible.

I have cared for many individuals who have survived such ordeals. For some, continued life has a meaning that far overshadows the suffering they experienced. Memory can be kind, and traces of the pain and humiliation that often accompany intensive medical treatment can fade as normal life resumes. For others who emerge from the treatment with major losses in function and independence, the process that they went through is often perceived ambivalently at best. Some wish they could have died rather than been forced to adjust to their unwanted dependence and disability, whereas others adjust and continue to find value in their life in spite of extraordinary burdens and limitations. I have given up trying to predict individuals' reactions and requests based on my own perception of their quality of life. Some individuals whose continued suffering appears overwhelming to me will eagerly fight death again no matter what the odds and requirements. Others whose quality of life and independence seem outstanding to me refuse all future invasive medical interventions. Since each individual's wishes and expectations are difficult if not impossible to predict accurately, it becomes of paramount importance for patients to be fully informed about their condition, the odds, and the nature of the interventions contemplated, so they can let their wishes be known.

I believe that options such as comfort care, which protect

severely ill patients from invasive medical treatments, should be offered to patients much earlier in the course of their illness. Such discussions initiate a dialogue whereby a patient can be encouraged to take a realistic look into the future, and begin to exercise some choice and control. Exploring the option of comfort care does not mean giving up, nor does it mean imposing it as a philosophy. It does, however, help the patient think clearly about the goals and potential outcomes of continued medical treatment. It opens the possibility of an alternative approach to care, in which alleviating suffering is given primary attention, instead of allowing suffering to be tolerated as an inevitable side effect of medicine's unquestioned effort to prolong life.

PATIENT CHOICE

Patients clearly have the right to fight for life even when the odds are poor. Consider Mr. W., an elderly patient of one of my partners, who had a widely spread cancer and coronary artery disease. In spite of his incurable illnesses and the extremely poor odds of success, Mr. W. still wanted to receive cardiopulmonary resuscitation should his heart cease beating. At first glance, this might seem like an irrational request. Yet on further exploration, it turned out that Mr. W. had previously survived a cardiac arrest. Given his heart disease, it was still possible that he could experience a disturbance in heart rhythm that could be relatively easily reversed with cardiopulmonary resuscitation. Resuscitation was therefore not completely futile, though the odds of it helping were very remote. Furthermore, since he had previously been through cardiopulmonary resuscitation, he was making a more informed decision than most patients.

In exploring the values and goals that underlay his decision, Mr. W.'s physician discovered that he had survived a forced labor camp in World War II. There he learned that one cannot give up no matter what the odds nor how poor the prognosis. For him, giving up on cardiopulmonary resuscitation meant giving in to hopelessness and despair. To stop fighting even against overwhelming odds was unacceptable to Mr. W., given his background and experience. His physician acquiesced after a thorough exploration, but did not stop there. He determined that if Mr. W. survived cardiopulmonary resuscitation but became permanently unconscious with no prospect of recovery, then Mr. W. would *not* want to be kept alive on machines. By continuing to explore and understand what his patient was trying to achieve, Mr. W.'s physician was able to give him the freedom both to request and to set limits on invasive medical care. He was not coerced into giving up his fight—a move that would have deprived his last days of meaning and direction. But he also did not have to risk being kept alive indefinitely on medical machines in order to achieve his goals.

Shortly after these discussions, Mr. W. experienced a cardiac arrest at home. Attempts to resuscitate him were unsuccessful.

WHAT HAPPENS IF I LOSE MENTAL CAPACITY?

Dying is frequently prolonged in patients who lose the mental capacity to let their wishes be known. All too often such patients have successfully avoided thinking about death and disability before losing mental competence, and they have not left clear directives to their family and physician. Family members often have ambivalent relationships with one another and with the patient, which make letting go and not "doing everything" much more difficult. The guilt that clouds a family member's judgment can be aggravated by being asked the wrong question by physicians. When asked: "What do *you* want us to do for your mother?" the answer is usually clear: "Everything possible." This generally translates into continued aggressive, life-prolonging medical treatments no matter what the odds, prognosis, or perceived quality of life. The family's chances of finding a more appropriate answer are enhanced by changing the emphasis of the question to: "What would *your mother* want us to do?" Asking the second question shifts the challenge to ascertaining the mother's values and wishes rather than the family's. The ethical principle underlying this approach is called "substituted judgment." The distinction is fundamental in helping families and other health-care agents understand their role in making medical decisions on behalf of incompetent persons. The patient's wishes and values are reaffirmed and protected by insisting on hearing the substantiating data upon which substituted judgments are based.

When there is any doubt about patients' wishes or their prognosis, medical practitioners almost always err on the side of aggressive medical treatment. There is a "presumption to treat" in medical care that protects physicians if they initiate emergency, potentially life-saving medical treatment in good faith on a patient in an emergency without that patient's knowledge or prior agreement. However, the presumption that all patients consent to medical treatment when their wishes are not known must be rethought in the case of the severely ill and the dying. Many times medical professionals feel forced to continue invasive medical treatments on patients whose wishes cannot be inferred with certainty, even when the effectiveness of such treatments is poor and the burdens are high. When such patients lose the mental capacity to refuse treatment, unless they have family or friends to advocate strongly on their behalf, the medical mandate to prolong life often takes over. Tragically, considerations about patients' suffering and the burdens of their treatment are often invalidated when one loses mental competence. The result can be repeated admissions to hospitals where well-intentioned medical care is gradually transformed into Chi-Chi, and dying becomes an elongated, undignified ordeal for patients who have lost the ability to say, "Stop!"

These profound life-and-death issues and uncertainties are difficult to grasp, and many people would prefer to avoid them. Yet they do so at their peril if they are unfortunate enough to lose their own capacity to make decisions. Without knowledge of patients' medical philosophy about end-of-life treatment, doctors must often repeatedly subject them to life-prolonging medical intervention no matter what their quality of life or prognosis. Although I agree with initially erring on the side of treatment under uncertain circumstances, medical professionals must do a better job of addressing the counterbalancing Hippocratic mandate to alleviate human suffering. To help patients, families, and health-care surrogates make good decisions, medical professionals need to be far more realistic and honest about the potential burdens of treatment, the odds of surviving fully intact, and the odds of surviving with a major added disability. Humane alternatives to invasive medical care need to be openly explored with patients and families, so that the goals and methods of treatment are realistically tailored to each patient's values and stage of illness.

People who are concerned or fearful about these matters must actively explore and develop their own end-of-life philosophy, and then clearly let it be known to their doctors and family members. As we shall see in Chapters 9 and 10, it is important formally to select, inform, and empower a Health Care Proxy who can help make medical decisions on your behalf should you lose competence in the future, or else formally express your goals and philosophy in the form of a Living Will. Without expressing your wishes clearly in advance, chances are you may not be allowed to go "gentle into that good night" as you face death should you lose the mental capacity to advocate for yourself. Instead, you will likely be forced to "rage, rage against the dying of the light," fighting death with invasive medical technology no matter how poor the odds or how high the personal costs. Under such circumstances, Chi-Chi can be a much more frightening enemy than death.

Chapter 4

COMFORT CARE

A Humane Alternative

omfort care is a humane approach to the medical treatment of incurably ill patients that embodies a set of principles, values, and techniques that are quite distinct from traditional medical care. Comfort care focuses its energy more on the patient's quality of life, personal meaning, and symptom alleviation than on prolonging life or treating disease. Given the dual directives of the Hippocratic Oath, comfort care clearly dedicates itself to alleviating patient suffering. The terms "comfort care," "hospice care," and "palliative care" are used interchangeably to capture this approach and philosophy. Comfort care is generally discussed and initiated under two circumstances: (1) when traditional medical treatments of a patient's disease are no longer effective; or (2) when the burdens of the patient's illness outweigh the benefits of continued aggressive medical treatment.

Although a comfort-care philosophy can be implemented in any clinical setting, it is most commonly associated with formal hospice programs. A hospice program is the institutional expression of comfort care, sometimes in the form of a residential facility devoted to the care of the dying, and other times in a formal program designed to provide comfort-care services in the patient's own home. Formal hospice programs began in England in the late 1960s with the founding of St. Christopher's Hospice in London. Initially they emphasized inpatient care of the terminally ill—patients were admitted to a residential facility, where they received comfort care from an attentive, multidisciplinary team of caregivers until they died. Hospice programs have proliferated in the last twenty years, both in the United Kingdom and in the United States, and they now provide a wide range of residential and home-based services. In the United States, the emphasis has been on providing comfort care in the patient's own home.

My own involvement was as a medical director of a Medicare-certified hospice program in Rochester, New York, where a wide range of health-care services and social supports could be provided, using a comfort-oriented philosophy within patients' own homes. In our hospice and in many like it in other communities, the patient's primary physician and the primary hospice nurse coordinated the patient's care. The resources of a team that includes social workers, nurses, volunteers, clergy, and a physician consultant can be drawn upon, depending on a given patient's condition and needs. Unlike a residential hospice, home hospice does not provide twenty-four-hour supervision, and considerable responsibility is placed on family members and friends to provide a large proportion of the patient's physical and emotional care. Applying a comfort-oriented approach to a patient's medical care does not require a formal hospice program, though the resources that become available in such programs can mean that the plan becomes more sophisticated and comprehensive.

The comfort-care philosophy can be used to guide treatment in any setting, including an acute hospital. However, it is most commonly offered by physicians only after all possibly effective medical treatments have been completely exhausted and the patient is near death. It is less frequently explored with patients whose quality of life is deteriorating, and whose burdens from acute medical treatments are increasing. The latter considerations are more subjective and personal, and are dependent on the patient's own experience, views, and values. By exploring truly distinct approaches to treatment such as comfort care earlier in a patient's illness, and by being more honest about traditional medicine's potential and limitations, patients can be given more control and choice about their treatment. The decision to continue trying every possible life-prolonging medical treatment no matter what the odds or side effects should be the result of a process of informed consent. There is nothing inherently preferable about an aggressive medical approach or a comfort-oriented strategy. The choice should belong to the patient.

Comfort care involves distinct trade-offs and priorities compared to traditional medical care. In traditional medical care, increased suffering is reluctantly accepted as a side effect of treatment that is directed primarily at extending the patient's life. In comfort care, unintended shortening of a patient's life can be accepted as a potential side effect of treatment, provided the primary purpose of the treatment is to relieve suffering. The underlying religious and ethical principle is called the "double effect," which absolves physicians from responsibility for indirectly contributing to the patient's death, provided they intended purely to alleviate the patient's symptoms. It places considerable weight on the physician's unambiguous intent to relieve suffering and not to intentionally shorten life.

Accepting the double effect in the care of the terminally ill has humanized and substantially improved the quality of life before death for many patients. It has freed doctors to use narcotic pain relievers so that they can effectively treat severe physical pain without fear of being morally or legally accountable if that treatment inadvertently contributes to an earlier death. Comfort care promises to humanize the process of dying, and to focus medical attention more on improving the quality than the quantity of the time remaining. In practice, comfort care allows physicians to use their considerable personal and professional resources to attend to the patient's suffering with the same intensity that they apply to prolonging the patient's life in traditional medical care.

Another fundamental difference between comfort care and traditional medical care is the relative emphasis given to the *patient as a person* compared to the patient's underlying disease. In the intensive-care unit, which represents the extreme of traditional medical care, invasive, often painful measures are used to monitor and treat a patient's underlying disease. Although every attempt is usually made to treat the person respectfully, the disease is the primary focus, not the patient. Comfort care, in contrast, involves the intensive care of the person. Treatment of the underlying disease is only relevant in how it contributes to the patient's overall quality of life. All treatments, procedures, and routines directed at the disease that do not directly contribute to the patient's comfort and personal integrity are discontinued. Treatment of uncomfortable sensations and symptoms takes clear precedence over treatment of the underlying disease.

For some physicians, the comfort-care philosophy threatens deeply held traditional medical values. Many see their primary professional mission as fighting for life, and easing the passage toward death has no place in that fight. Physicians are also much more skilled and better trained to care for patients by treating their underlying diseases than by addressing the complex, often idiosyncratic elements of their suffering. In training, physicians have been repeatedly warned about the dangers of oversedation and addiction that can accompany the use of narcotic pain relievers. In emergency departments and intensive-care units, physicians must at times anesthetize themselves from the intense suffering around them in order to do their primary job. Rarely if ever is time taken for physicians to explore personally the anguish that they see on a daily basis. It is little surprise that the alternative of comfort care is offered late if at all to severely ill patients, and that the physicians' commitment to relieving suffering in the terminally ill is often less strong than the energy devoted to treating diseases in traditional medical settings.

Comfort care values the uniqueness of each human being, and tries to individualize as much as possible. There are therefore no preset formulas about how to proceed until one has met the patient and begun to understand what is important from his perspective. Comfort care tries to give each individual maximum control, making no assumptions about what choices might be made. Some patients may have strong fears about the use of narcotic medications, whereas others may fear the potential of uncontrolled pain. One patient may want to die at home no matter what, and another may prefer to stay at home until the end is near, but then return to the hospital to die. Some individuals may easily accept their family's involvement in intimate bodily care as they become weaker, whereas others may find such dependence humiliating and unacceptable. For each decision, the values and expectations of the patient must take precedence over those of the caregivers and the family. Although medicine now has reasonably effective measures for relieving cancer pain and other symptoms, we cannot assume that any comfort-oriented treatment will be acceptable to a given patient without informing him and gaining his consent.

The physician using a comfort-oriented approach needs to learn about new techniques for symptom treatment. Potent concentrated liquid and sustained-release narcotic pain relievers are available to relieve pain. It has been clearly demonstrated that giving these medications at regular intervals around the clock, rather then waiting for the pain to intensify before taking them, provides better relief for chronic pain. Alternative delivery systems are now available for patients who are unable to swallow or tolerate oral medications. For example, substantial relief can be achieved by using topical narcotic skin patches, and highly concentrated pain relievers can be delivered subcutaneously, using a small, easily portable pump that can be attached to the patient's belt. It is beyond the scope of this book to describe all the new techniques available to relieve pain or other physical symptoms.* But physicians must become more knowledgeable about and skilled at comfort care, and they must seek the help of persons experienced in the care of the terminally ill when faced with what seem to be intractable symptomatic problems.

The context in which a comfort-care plan is developed not only involves the values, expectations, and condition of the patient, but usually also the family. A comfort-oriented philosophy tries to enhance direct personal interaction between the patient and the significant people in his or her life. Though the patient clearly should have ultimate control about how to involve the family, each family member may have beliefs and expectations about the patient, the disease, and the treatment that ideally should be voiced and understood. For some families, the period before a patient's death can be a time for connection and resolution of outstanding conflicts. For others, it aggravates long-standing family problems that continue to distress the dying person. In either case, those caring for the dying want to maximize the potential for individual and family healing, and to minimize the added suffering that may emanate from unresolvable family conflicts. Health-care providers and friends may have a vision about how families should move through this process and work out unresolved issues before the patient dies, but it is extremely important to allow families and especially the patient as much flexibility and control as possible. I generally encourage family meetings with the central caretakers and the patient present, but I have seen enough difficult family circumstances to know that the patient should have ultimate control about how this should proceed, if at all.

*Readers may wish to see the Bibliography on p. 244 for some references on this topic.

Many patients have a specific fear that haunts them as they contemplate the end of life. That fear often feels so intimate and personal that it is frightening even to give voice to it. Sharing such fears with another person requires considerable trust and courage. Sometimes the fear, once explored and understood, is relatively easy to relieve. For example, many patients fear dying while overwhelmed by physical pain, or dependent on medical technologies like breathing machines or feeding tubes. Using a comfort-care philosophy, physicians can be reassuring about those two concerns. First, patients on comfort care are protected from cardiopulmonary resuscitation by having "do-not-resuscitate" orders. If these interventions are inadvertently initiated by medical personnel for any reason, they can be immediately discontinued as soon as the patient's wishes are known. A comfort-care philosophy also allows us to reassure those who fear dying in severe physical pain. I can honestly promise that I will continue to increase medications until the pain is relieved, even if the patient has to be medicated to the point of unconsciousness to achieve this end, and even if that inadvertently shortens life. For a patient who has witnessed death marked by severe uncontrolled pain or dependence on medical technology, such promises can be helpful.

For patients like Diane who fear loss of control, dependence on others for their intimate physical care, or a life devoid of personally meaningful activity, the promises of comfort care are often less reassuring. Exploring a terminally ill person's fears about dying does not necessarily imply an obligation or ability to resolve them. Such fears are present whether or not the physician, caretakers, or family know about them. But by encouraging a patient to share these concerns, the isolation is lessened, and the possibility of a more open, honest discussion is revealed. A thorough exploration of such sensitive ground can also sometimes yield alternatives for understanding and meaning—new options might emerge from this painful discussion. Our wish as caretakers to resolve what may be unresolvable often inhibits us from opening up difficult areas, such as a patient's true fears about death or dying. Yet, even when the patient's problems are insoluble, such explorations are central to further humanizing our comfort-oriented approach to the end of life.

The physician, too, may have unstated fears and unexpressed feelings. Perhaps the patient reminds her of her parent who died a painful death, leaving her feeling both impotent and enraged. Perhaps too many patients have died recently, and she is beginning to question her decision to go into medicine, which she had hoped would be filled more with recovery and gratitude than with loss and grief. Perhaps she has so identified with this patient that she can feel the impending death as her own, and begins to ponder the frightening inevitability of her own mortality. Perhaps she secretly agrees with her patient that death is no longer the enemy, and fears that the patient may ask her for active assistance in dying, not knowing how she will respond. Like their patients, doctors too have to find a safe outlet for their secret thoughts and fears. Without expressing and sharing them, physicians themselves can become isolated and depressed. Because their fears can also be unique and private, they should probably be explored with trusted colleagues and friends rather than patients. They may or may not reflect feelings shared by the patient, but unless they are clearly relevant and helpful to the patient, they are better worked through outside of the doctor-patient relationship.

Perhaps the most fundamental commitment that physicians make to their dying patients is not to abandon them, no matter how the last stages of their illness may unfold. For many, the fear of dying can be equated with a fear that one will face unspeakable, unknown problems alone at the end. Not only is the actual experience of death unknowable, but the path one will take to get there is also filled with fear and uncertainty. Knowing that you will have an experienced guide or partner who will not abandon you, no matter how difficult the terrain, can be reassuring. It does not guarantee an easy time, or definite answers, but it gives assurance that you will not have to struggle alone. Comfort care allows the physician to use her own personal resources and medicine's considerable power to help her patient by enhancing meaning and lessening suffering prior to death. While it does not guarantee a dignified, pain-free death, it is a promise to continue to try to enhance the patient's dignity, control, and sense of choice before death, no matter where illness may take them both. It may require as much courage, creativity, and stamina for the physician to face this uncertainty as it does to treat the sickest patient in the medical intensive-care unit. Facing this unknown with dying patients is one of the richest, most rewarding challenges in medicine. Our dying patients have no choice about facing death; perhaps the greatest gift of comfort care is that they don't have to face it alone.

W E N D Y

Wendy was thirty-seven years old. She had had ovarian cancer for the past five years. When I became her doctor she was nearing the end of a medical odyssey, including over twenty hospitalizations for surgery, chemotherapy, and multiple infections. Fortunately, Wendy had also experienced long periods of a relatively normal, high-quality life to balance these intense, very unpleasant medical experiences. In recent months, however, her pain, dependency, nausea, and vomiting began to outweigh her enjoyment. Her cancer specialists had run out of treatments that had any reasonable chance of working. The cancer had spread throughout her abdomen and chest, and she had a huge open wound that would not heal and required frequent dressing changes. She could not eat, and was kept alive by continuous intravenous feeding through a catheter that went directly into a vein in the center of her body. Her pain was intense, and poorly con-

trolled. Wendy had decided that she never wanted to return to the hospital again. She had reached an impasse with her cancer specialists about this issue, and was referred to me as a primary-care physician with an interest in hospice care. Although I usually served as a consultant rather than the primary physician for hospice patients, her story was compelling enough for me to make an exception.

Knowing about her ominous medical condition, I knocked on her door with some trepidation. To my surprise, a remarkably attractive young woman dressed in sweatpants answered. Expecting to be taken to a deathbed, I soon learned that she was the patient. After hearing more about her experiences and her wishes, it was clear to me that her death was not necessarily imminent, nor was she ready to die. She did want to halt the added discomfort and pain imposed by further chemotherapy or surgery. Yet, Wendy definitely wanted to continue living as long as possible provided her life had sufficient quality to be meaningful to her. Her biggest fear was being kept alive by intravenous feedings if she permanently lost her mental capacity. I was able to guarantee Wendy that I would stop these treatments and allow her to die should she enter into a coma or become irreversibly incompetent.

As we addressed her symptoms from a comfort-oriented perspective, it became clear that the unrelenting abdominal pain and the foul smell that emanated from her wound were her biggest unresolved problems. Because she already had a permanent indwelling intravenous catheter for feedings, the uncontrolled pain was relatively easily solved by a continuous infusion of morphine. Within a few days what had been a preoccupying and disabling problem was now under control. Without severe pain, she was able to be much more active. It was less clear how to decrease the smell from her wound, which was filled with extensive cancer growth, so that the prospects of its healing were remote. Because I had no special expertise about this type of wound care, I consulted with several experienced hospice nurses. They came up with creative suggestions which, through a process of trial and error, gradually brought the odor under enough control that

Wendy could have guests into her home and occasionally go out without feeling self-conscious. Despite the fact that we could not influence the progression of her underlying disease, her quality of life improved dramatically once her physical symptoms were carefully addressed.

The complexity of Wendy's intravenous feedings and wound dressings had necessitated that she move back home with her parents. Her independence from her parents had been hard fought, so the return to her childhood home and an unacknowledged dependence upon her parents were very unsettling. Wendy and her parents did not talk openly with each other about the severity of her illness and the nearness of death, though they were each willing to talk about it in private. Despite my recommendation to Wendy that I meet with them as a family to try to establish more open communication, she convinced me that she was not ready for that type of intimacy with her parents. Wendy did allow me to meet with her parents and ensure that they knew the severity of her medical condition. It turned out that Wendy's family was aware of her prognosis, and were respectful and even relieved that Wendy did not want to discuss it directly with them.

Wendy lived for four more months in relative comfort, including surviving two rather severe infections with the help of intravenous antibiotics administered at home by the hospice nurses. Though it might seem inconsistent that life-prolonging treatments like potent antibiotics are used as a part of comfort care, Wendy wanted to continue living as long as possible provided she could stay out of the hospital. She appreciated being given a choice about the limited options she had left, and did not want any assumptions to be made about what she would and would not want.

Wendy subsequently became much weaker and eventually could not get out of bed. Even rolling over onto her side to have the bed linens changed became a painful ordeal, in spite of substantial increases in her intravenous pain medicines. She was now sleeping much of the time. When awake, she began to speak repeatedly and *clearly about her readiness to die. We discussed whether her intrave-nous fluids were now contributing to comfort or prolonging her suffering, and Wendy decided that she wanted them discontinued. She was withdrawing from other people at this point, and the deci-sion from her perspective was not even a sad one. It was as if she had already left. Had we continued her intravenous fluids, Wendy might have lingered on the edge of death for weeks or longer.*

For her parents, Wendy's emotional withdrawal was very painful. Though they did not like to talk explicitly about Wendy's dying, they were very deeply connected and devoted to her. Her return home, even under these tragic circumstances, had brought new life and meaning into the household. Her death would leave them feeling empty and grief-stricken. In our discussions, they were willing to learn about the futility of her current medical situation, and about Wendy's wishes and fears about the future. Eventually they were able to see her withdrawal as part of her inevitable exit from this life, not as a personal rejection. After a terribly sad but courageous con-versation, they accepted Wendy's decision to discontinue her intra-venous fluids. Intravenous morphine in doses sufficient to control the pain was the only treatment that remained. Wendy slipped into a coma and died seventy-two hours later, her parents sitting at her side.

Wendy's parents and I were saddened by her death, perhaps as much for ourselves as for her. We each enjoyed and benefited in different ways from being with her during the final phase of her life. We all took strength from Wendy's courage. We also agreed that trying to prolong her life any further would have been more for our sakes than for hers. At the end, Wendy felt she had only suffering to look forward to.

Using the techniques of comfort care, Wendy had four months of very high quality time even though death was near. She avoided a return to the hospital, and was an active participant in all the medical decisions. Once we had helped to relieve her physical symptoms, she was able to spend more of her limited energy interacting with family and friends. At her death, when quality and meaning were rapidly disappearing, the same comfort-care principles helped to facilitate a relatively simple and pain-free passage into death. By discontinuing her intravenous feedings when they were no longer contributing to her comfort, Wendy was allowed to die over several days by passing into a coma without outward signs of struggle or discomfort. For many patients, when the end of life is near or when suffering is severe, comfort care provides the principles for making some very difficult decisions. It can allow physicians to provide much more meaning, control, and dignity for dying patients than they can by continuing traditional medical care.

M R S. J.

Mrs. J. was a Holocaust survivor. She had lost her entire family in the concentration camps, and had rebuilt her life in Europe after the war, where she worked as a seamstress until retirement. She had recently come to the United States with her husband of thirty years to be near their children. She had known pain and suffering, and did not give in easily to either. Five years earlier she had been diagnosed with colon cancer and was treated with surgery followed by chemo-therapy. When I first met Mrs. J., she came to my office in a wheel-chair—a reluctant concession to the excruciating pain that she was having in her back and down her right leg. Mrs. J. had been in pain for over six months, but the fear that her cancer had recurred kept her from seeking medical help. Finally the pain became too much even for her. Unfortunately, her fear was well founded. A scan of the lower back and abdomen showed extensive cancer spread, including involvement of the nerves to the right leg. After exploring the op-tions, we agreed to admit her to the hospital to try to get her pain under control and to begin radiation therapy to her back and pelvic area. We knew that this treatment would not cure her cancer, and probably not even prolong her life; but we hoped it could relieve her pain so that the time she had left would be of higher quality.

Mrs. J. was a very stoic woman who had strong negative feelings about narcotic pain medicines. Her instincts told her that she should wait until her pain was unbearable before taking such medication, though these peaks of pain were undermining any sense of well-being that remained. The fear of pain began to dominate her thoughts. After several serious negotiations, she agreed to a trial of regular dosing around the clock, which eventually took the extreme peaks out of her pain and allowed her to focus more of her attention on other things. The radiation also helped, and with less pain she was again able to walk short distances. In spite of this progress, both Mrs. J. and I knew that the cancer would be back in the future, forcing us to face more difficult and unwanted dilemmas. Since there are no traditional medical treatments that are proven to be effective at this stage of colon cancer (she had already tried and failed the one form of chemotherapy that has some effectiveness), the options we explored included a comfort-oriented approach or experimental chemotherapy. Mrs. J. felt that she had already suffered too much to try experimental treatment (in fact, such treatments had very special, terrifying meaning to her, given her experience in World War II), so she sadly selected comfort care. Arrangements were made to enroll her in our community's hospice program.

Mrs. J. spent the next two months at home with her husband and children. Her pain was under control with relatively low doses of medication. We subsequently learned that the pain was much worse when she was alone, and that she feared being abandoned and left alone even more than she feared pain. Luckily, Mrs. J. had a large, supportive family, so by carefully scheduling and coordinating visit times we were able to keep people around her almost all of the time. She was not a person who asked for help easily, so on her own she would not have asked for these regular visits, but she clearly relished them. They did more good than any other intervention to maintain her spirit, and to alleviate her fears.

Eventually, the pain in Mrs. J.'s right leg returned with a vengeance. She became bedbound, and needed much higher doses of pain-relieving medication. The side effects of increased medication were confusion and sedation, so that the quality of her family contact deteriorated. When she was alert enough to converse with her family, she was distracted by the severe pain. When she had enough medicine to be out of pain, she was too sedated to enjoy their presence fully. Since the cancer had yet to invade and threaten any vital organs, it was unlikely that death would provide an imminent escape.

As Mrs. J.'s physician, I cast a broad net looking for alternatives for achieving pain control. She had already had a maximum dose of radiation and had not responded to chemotherapy. I discussed the situation with a neurosurgeon, who suggested the possibility of making a small cut in her spinal cord, thereby blocking the transmission of pain sensation from the affected area to the brain. An unfortunate but certain by-product of this treatment would be the complete and irreversible paralysis of her right leg. Under ordinary circumstances, such a severe adverse side effect would be unacceptable; but Mrs. J. was already unable to walk, and the quality of her life was becoming so poor that it seemed worth exploring. There were no good alternatives, and this seemed to be the best of those available.

When I presented the idea to Mrs. J. and her family, they unhesitatingly jumped at the chance. Living in such pain was a nightmare for them all, and the possibility of an escape no matter what the potential consequences was worth considering. The trade-off of not walking seemed minuscule to them when compared with the certainty of continued excruciating pain without the procedure. We made arrangements to admit her to the hospital the next day.

The next problem that I encountered was from the hospital staff, who felt uncomfortable with the high amounts of pain medicines Mrs. J. was taking. They were concerned about addiction, and about the potential for legal and professional liability if they gave such high *doses of narcotics that she developed a problem. Some were also skeptical about using such invasive surgery on a terminally ill person. After a meeting in which I heard their concerns and informed them in more depth about the evolution of Mrs. J.'s illness and the principles of comfort care on which her treatment decisions were based, the staff became more comfortable with the plan. The surgery went smoothly and the results were dramatic. Though Mrs. J. could not move her leg, her pain was almost completely relieved. We were able to cut back drastically on the pain medicine. She returned home in two days a new person. Mrs. J. and her family felt we had performed a miracle.*

Mrs. J. lived an additional two months relatively free of pain. Her family continued their regularly scheduled visits. She felt secure that she would never have to be alone. It was a time filled with intense joy and sadness for the entire family. Because the cancer spread extensively into her abdomen, Mrs. J. eventually lost the ability to eat. She did not want intravenous or tube feedings. Instead, her family learned to fix tiny meals of her favorite foods, and she savored the tastes and smells. She became weaker and weaker, and gradually went into a coma. Mrs. J. died a relatively peaceful death, with her family in constant attendance. Her fear that she would be abandoned was never realized, and her excruciating pain was controlled using both orthodox and unorthodox methods.

I present Mrs. J.'s story to illustrate that there is nothing formulaic about comfort care. Like traditional medical care, an individual patient's course is often filled with difficult and uncertain decisions that should be fully shared and explored. Comfort care does not necessarily exclude invasive medical measures, as long as the goal of the intervention is relieving symptoms and improving the patient's overall quality of life, and the patient finds it acceptable. Comfort care is as creative and challenging as traditional medical care, only the course is much more tailored to and defined by the specific patient and the discomfort rather than the underlying disease.

STOPPING TREATMENT

Some patients who are dependent on life-sustaining treatments reach a point in their illness when continued living has no meaning and makes no sense. In essence, these patients choose death rather than continued dependence on medical treatments. Discontinuing life supports can sometimes be a part of the decision to pursue a comfort-oriented approach to treatment. Though it is important to ensure that the patient's judgment is not distorted by depression or other mental illness, it is generally accepted that the request to discontinue life-sustaining treatments can be rational, and should be addressed seriously and openly by the physician. Patients frequently begin such treatments in uncertain medical circumstances when they are mentally competent and in relatively good physical condition; then, over time, their state of health and their quality of life changes radically, so that the original goals and the methods of treatment must be reanalyzed.

The shift from traditional medical care to comfort care can have dramatic, immediately apparent consequences for patients who are dependent on life-sustaining treatment. Many such treatments are invasive and can be very uncomfortable for patients. They can be justified for patients who have an otherwise good quality of life or prospect for recovery, or when started in an uncertain clinical situation. Yet patients or their families can request that they be discontinued if the prospect for recovery worsens and the burdens of treatment outweigh the benefits. If the treatment is a mechanical ventilator, the patient dependent upon it may die within minutes or hours if it is discontinued. The resulting symptoms of shortness of breath can be relieved with morphine even in doses that may inadvertently hasten the patient's death, provided the goal is to relieve suffering and not to produce death. If another patient is receiving regular dialysis treatments for kidney failure, then discontinuing dialysis will be accompanied by death within approximately a week or ten days. This patient is likely to slip into a coma over that time, and the symptoms associated with fluid or toxin accumulation can be lessened with appropriate comfort-oriented measures. Estimates vary considerably, but anywhere from 2 to 25 percent of patients on kidney dialysis die as a result of voluntary discontinuation of treatment, depending on the center and the method of reporting.

In the United States, patients clearly have the right to refuse any treatment, even if the treatment is life-sustaining or life-saving. Before making such a vital decision, it is important that all alternatives have been explored in depth and understood by the patient. Such decisions should never be distorted by inadequate treatment of potentially reversible problems (i.e., inadequate treatment of chronic pain), nor should they be colored by a depression that may be treatable. Yet, once such reversible problems are excluded, the physician must take the patient's request seriously. Such rational requests are not uncommon. In fact, an American Hospital Association survey estimates that approximately six thousand deaths every day are in some way planned in the United States. Once the decision is reached to discontinue life-sustaining treatment, then all patient care should be guided by a comfort-oriented philosophy.

M R. P.

Mr. P.'s disease is many people's worst fear: a malignant brain tumor. His tumor involved the parietal lobe—that part of the brain that partially controls complex thinking and connections between ideas. His cancer was first identified when he had a seizure. At that time he had no headache or any other sign that his brain was not working properly. His neurological examination showed only very subtle abnormalities that were not interfering in any way with his usual mental or physical functioning. The brain biopsy showed a very malignant cancer, and treatment with a combination of surgery, radiation, and chemotherapy was recommended. Mr. P. was a wonderful, easygoing person with tremendous faith in medicine, and he unhesitatingly went forward with the treatment on all fronts. He emerged from surgery with more difficulty doing complex cognitive tasks (calculations, reading, and writing), but his warm sense of humor allowed him to compensate for and hide his deficits. Initially, Mr. P. was able to ignore his disease most of the time, and continue with a relatively normal life.

Several months later, however, he began to be bothered by complex hallucinations, and his thinking about routine daily matters was invaded by strange, extraneous thoughts. He also developed a steady, boring headache that would not let up. A repeat scan of his brain showed that the cancer was again growing, so we started a medication to try to lessen the brain swelling. His headache improved, but his thinking continued to be disturbed. This mild-mannered, easygoing person was now regularly troubled by agitation, sleeplessness, and fear of those around him. He was temporarily admitted to the psychiatric floor of the hospital to try to get his disturbing symptoms under better control. He had times of extraordinary clarity of mind, when he would clearly state that he would rather be dead than live like this. Our psychiatric consultant felt that this wish was rational, given his extremely poor quality of life, the fact that he understood his disease and the treatment options available, and the absence of a treatable or distorting depression. We made repeated adjustments in psychiatric and anti-seizure medications to try to get his symptoms under better control. Some of the treatments seemed to help, but all who could bear to look would agree with Mr. P. that he was living a nightmare.

Arrangements were made to admit Mr. P. to our home hospice

program. Mr. P. had always been a central, dominating figure in his family. His children had difficulty understanding why he could not get better and return to being the father they had known and loved. After several family meetings, they began to acknowledge how sick he was, but they refused to listen to or explore his repeated statements that he wished he were dead rather than continuing to live in such an intolerable condition. Life at home was very difficult in spite of hospice support and an attentive family. Mr. P. continued to fluctuate between hours and even days of extraordinary mental clarity when he could make contact with his family, and periods of agitation and frightening hallucinations when he would feel threatened by those around him. He repeatedly stated his wish to die.

Mr. P. lived in a small home on the shore of Lake Ontario. One winter afternoon when he was left alone for a few moments, he ran out over the ice in an attempt to dive into the freezing waters of the lake. His son spotted him and made a life-saving tackle as he neared the edge of the water. Subsequently, his family kept a continuous twenty-four-hour vigil to ensure that this would not happen again. Mr. P. now felt trapped, with no escape and no options.

Several weeks later, he was again admitted to the hospital because of recurrent seizures. In periods of mental clarity, Mr. P. reiterated his view that continued life was his enemy, not death. As we struggled to find some acceptable options either to help his symptoms or to ease his death, we realized that the steroids he was taking for his brain swelling were in fact prolonging his life, and that he could choose to discontinue them and die within a few hours or days. When given this information, without hesitation Mr. P. requested that they be discontinued and that he be allowed to die with what little dignity remained to him. I assured myself that Mr. P. knew what he was requesting, though I knew it was what he had been praying for. I discussed the decision with his family and with the hospital staff. When forced to look at the choice from Mr. P.'s perspective, they reluctantly agreed.

Within twelve hours after the steroids were discontinued, Mr. P.

*was in a deep coma, and one day later he died. We were all saddened
by his death and somewhat unsettled by our role in indirectly facilitating it; still, we also knew in our hearts that continued life under
these abhorrent circumstances was worse for him than death. By
thinking carefully about each of our interventions to be sure they
were contributing to his quality of life, we were able to discontinue a
well-intentioned treatment that had outlived its usefulness, and was
now indirectly contributing to his suffering by prolonging his life.*

Comfort care provides a remarkably humane, effective alternative to traditional medical treatment in the care of the severely ill
and the dying. Paying primary attention to patients' quality of life
and to the alleviation of their suffering seems much more appropriate to this phase of life than a continued fight for life that is
blind to the personal consequences. The patient's values must
guide these decisions. But to make a rational choice, patients need
to be much more fully informed about their prognosis and about
comfort care as a viable alternative that means far more than
"giving up." Comfort care should be offered as a possibility much
earlier in the course of an incurable illness, for it can guide a very
humane approach to treatment for long periods of time. It is not
necessarily the last alternative, after all medical treatments with
even a remote possibility of helping have been tried and failed.
Rather, it is a philosophy of care that attends to personal suffering
more than medical disease. Comprehensively applied, comfort
care is usually able to ensure an adequately controlled, acceptably
dignified terminal phase of life. Rather than using medical technology to fight death to the end, comfort care allows us to use that
same creative energy and technology to alleviate suffering and
physical symptoms—goals that are likely to be more appropriate
when death is near. I agree fully with those who advocate for more
availability of both residential and home hospice care, but I also
know that in the interim, comfort care can be offered in any
setting provided the patient and the health-care providers are in

agreement about what they are trying to achieve. Over the last twenty years, the development and implementation of comfort care has proved a major achievement in using medical care to help severely ill patients die with more dignity, control, and support.

Chapter 5

THE LIMITATIONS OF COMFORT CARE

Double Effects, Double Binds, and Double Standards

Comfort care, properly and comprehensively applied, can ensure a dignified death for most incurably ill patients. Unfortunately, there are anguishing exceptions where severe end-of-life suffering still occurs. The unrelieved suffering that stems from inadequate utilization of comfort care, or as the result of the restricted availability of medical care in general and of hospice programs in particular, is unnecessary and potentially reversible. These problems should be solved by educating doctors and by increasing the allocation of economic resources to health care for the under-served and to comfort care for the dying. Other limitations posed by the insoluble physical, emotional, and existential dilemmas incurably ill persons have to face are not so readily correctable. One of our most troubling challenges as physicians and caregivers is to respond to these patients for whom comprehensively applied comfort care is unable to adequately relieve their suffering, so that death seems the only sensible escape.

CORRECTABLE LIMITATIONS

Some correctable limitations of comfort care have been mentioned in previous chapters. Comfort care is offered to too few patients, often very late in their illness, and only after all conceivable more aggressive medical interventions have been repeatedly tried and failed. It is usually presented as the last resort, with an apology that there is nothing more to do, rather than as a positive, humane alternative approach to the last phase of one's life. Doctors are generally much better trained to fight disease than to talk with patients about prognosis and the likelihood of death. The physician's ability to use the technical aspects of medicine is carefully monitored in training and as part of the credentialing process for being given hospital privileges; yet many physicians have never adequately developed the technical and interpersonal skills needed to provide comfort care. In teaching hospitals, most patients are no longer seen by medical students or residents when the decision is made to treat them with comfort care. It is felt to be a waste of the trainee's valuable time when they are "not going to do anything." "Not doing anything" translates into not undertaking traditional, disease-oriented medical treatments; but by implication it devalues the many complex medical options still available to help comfort the terminally ill. The clear message is given that caring for the dying has less importance than caring for those who will use medical technology to fight for life. Although there are voluntary workshops and courses for those who wish to learn how to better care for the dying, more often than not they are taken by those few who already possess considerable skill and understanding.

Many doctors complete their medical training without having developed the ability to communicate with their patients about death or about the limits of medical intervention. They may also lack the technical skills to provide pain and symptom relief for patients who are dying. Some physicians routinely undermedicate chronic pain even with terminally ill patients, partly because their training in pharmacology emphasizes the risks of overmedication, sedation, and addiction much more than the need to fully assess and relieve pain. Whereas these are legitimate and important concerns, they are far more relevant to the traditional medical care of patients with reversible medical problems than they are to the care of the terminally ill. Yet when I was the medical director of a hospice program, I frequently heard of physicians reinforcing rather than alleviating a dying patient's fears about addiction from narcotic pain relievers, and recommending that such medication be taken only when the pain was severe rather than preventively on a regular schedule around the clock.

The inability to talk with patients about the burdens of treatment, prognosis, death, and the option of comfort care is potentially remediable through proper education and training, though building up these skills requires supervised work with patients. The first time a doctor talks about these issues with a patient can be unsettling, and the direction taken in the interview often feels uncertain. It requires some basic redefinition of beliefs that a physician may have about always having the answers, or always providing definite solutions. The skills of listening and sharing decision making with patients are complex, and need to be developed over time. Unlike technical skill, which is carefully monitored both in training and in practice, medical educators have left the development of these communication skills largely to chance. The result is an extreme variability in doctors' willingness and ability to carry out such conversations. This is a potentially correctable problem, but it requires a commitment and understanding on behalf of medical schools and professional organizations that learning these interpersonal skills is just as important as learning technical skills. Currently, trainees are unequivocally given the opposite message.

The decision not to abandon patients when disease-oriented treatment becomes futile or too burdensome is fundamental to promoting a dignified death. The policy that medical trainees do not continue to care for hospitalized patients once they no longer receive aggressive medical interventions violates this principle. It is at this point, where traditional medical algorithms and decisions are no longer applicable, that comfort care begins. If we don't train physicians to talk with patients about what comfort care might mean, and under what circumstances it might be applicable, then they won't have even the rudimentary knowledge and skills needed to establish a comfort-oriented treatment plan. Furthermore, if we present trainees with the illusion that comfort care or a hospice can always ensure a humane, dignified death without their creative input, what are they going to do the first time a patient of theirs struggles before death in the face of their best efforts?

By creating the illusion that comfort care guarantees a dignified, acceptable death for all patients, we set up the potential for doctors and patients to become disconnected or distrustful at the critical moment when this illusion breaks down. Instead, we must encourage and support both training and practicing doctors to learn more from their patients about their fears, hopes, and experiences as they face death. The skills needed to talk about death, to explore all reasonable options for approaching it, and to avoid abandoning dying patients no matter how overwhelming their experience, are potentially reversible defects in our current system of medical training.

If some physicians choose to specialize exclusively in the more technical aspects of patient care, then it is vital for them to involve other professionals who can communicate with the patient. For example, if an oncologist sees his job as providing chemotherapy and fighting cancer, he may want to have the patient's primary-care physician stay intimately involved. That primary-care physician then provides a broader perspective, attending to the overall goals and to the personal aspects of the patient's illness.

Comfort care also includes technical treatments that physicians must learn. New methods for pain control have been developed, as have strategies for relieving other symptoms. Physicians treating severely ill patients must keep up with these new developments, or else involve others with special expertise when they encounter difficult problems with terminally ill patients. Since the ground rules for comfort care are so dependent on the individual patient, it is often useful to seek a second opinion when the direction becomes uncertain or symptoms appear unresolvable. If the patient is fortunate enough to be in a hospice program, a multidisciplinary team can often provide such consultation and advice. However, if comfort care is being provided in a different setting, the physician may have to seek formal or informal counsel from other experienced health-care providers, or experts in pain relief or symptom management, in order to ensure the patient's optimal comfort.

The final, reversible limitation of comfort care is in the financing and provision of hospices. Hospice care is currently a Medicare benefit, though some other insurers are beginning to include it. This benefit covers only those patients with proper insurance and a prognosis of less than six months, who have someone at home who can serve as a primary caregiver. The primary caregiver is responsible for the majority of care, supplemented as needed by professional and paraprofessional staff. This generally limits the benefit to patients with functioning, well-organized, caring families, though it has recently been expanded to include those who reside in nursing facilities. Those without such families or social supports, who often have even greater need, generally do not qualify. This is especially true for the millions of families in the United States who are currently under- or uninsured. Hospice is a wonderful benefit that can provide additional help for dying patients who wish to spend their remaining time at home. For those without adequate medical insurance or with limited social supports, however, the current benefits from hospices are more potential than real.

What are the options in the United States for inpatient hospice care? A substantial proportion of our escalating health-care costs is spent primarily on providing biotechnical care in the last phases of life. When a physician decides to stop the technical approach and shift to comfort care, insurers will often stop coverage because the hospitalization is no longer considered "acute." This sometimes creates an absurd situation in which expensive, unwanted technical treatments are continued in order to ensure continued insurance coverage. Some patients who might otherwise prefer a more comfortable, less expensive, less technical approach to the last stage of their illness may continue accepting futile medical treatments simply to guarantee continued insurance coverage. Physicians, too, are well reimbursed if they continue to perform invasive procedures, but the difficult conversations about the possibility of death and the option of comfort care are by and large not paid for. With such disproportionate financial incentives, it is no surprise that the possibility of comfort care is often left unexplored until all other medical options have been exhausted.

Inpatient hospice or comfort care in an acute-care hospital is equated by payers with long-term care, and is therefore only financially covered for those few with special long-term insurance policies. In New York State, there are a few privately funded, volunteer-staffed, two-bed residential hospices where free terminal care is provided, but the demand for such beds far outstrips their availability. Patients on Medicare-certified hospice programs can sometimes be admitted to an inpatient hospice for symptom control, or to give the family some respite, but here there is generally a time limit of one to two weeks. Inpatient hospice beds are highly restricted and controlled, unavailable to most of those whose need is greatest.

The restrictions on home and inpatient hospice care in the United States are clearly reversible limitations in our current efforts to provide comfort care. Accessible home hospice care and residential hospices for the terminally ill should be part of any national health plan. Given the extraordinary expenditures generated using medical technology in a futile fight against death in the last months of life, this might even cost less than is currently being spent. No matter what the economic impact, more awareness and availability of comfort care and hospice are clearly needed as we make decisions and set priorities in the care of the incurably ill.

IRREVERSIBLE LIMITATIONS

Each of the limitations presented so far is potentially reversible, provided we change our priorities in training physicians and in health-care reimbursement. This change in emphasis would clearly help many dying persons receive health care that is properly tailored to the last stages of life. Yet even on a hospice program with unlimited financial and personnel resources, there remain some troubling circumstances where intolerable suffering still occurs. Comfort care has developed sophisticated means of relieving physical suffering, but much of the angst that dying patients experience is more emotional and existential than simply physical. Dignity involves the integration of a person's physical, emotional, intellectual, and spiritual aspects; it is complex, and unique to each individual. Those who equate care of the dying simply with controlling physical symptoms implicitly devalue the personal experience of patients whose lives can gradually become devoid of everything that had meaning to them.

Diane, for example, lived very fully and independently on a hospice program, using comfort-care principles from her diagnosis to her death. While physical and emotional suffering was present, it was tolerable. With the assistance of her family, she was able fully to manage her own physical care. She initially came to my office for medical visits, but as she became weaker, I went to see her at her home. She was visited at least once each week by her hospice nurse. Despite the effectiveness of the hospice program, Diane still feared being out of control, bedbound, and totally dependent. She had an extreme aversion to lying passively in bed, to being unable to attend to her basic bodily functions, or to being sedated or confused while she waited for death. For her, such a state would have been far worse than being dead. Diane was able to live without being overly concerned or preoccupied that this fear would become a reality in part because she knew she could take her own life if it became unacceptable to her. Since her death was inevitable, she felt that going through such torment in the last moments of her life would have been meaningless and absurd. It would have undermined all that she was struggling to achieve.

Mr. P., the man with the brain tumor whose death was described in the last chapter, progressively lost core elements of how he defined himself as a person in spite of comprehensively applied comfort care. His dying was a nightmare, and death was the only way out. Ironically, the key to helping Mr. P. die with a modicum of dignity was my awakening to the idea that he could die by stopping use of the very medicine that was keeping him alive. My intention was clearly to relieve his suffering, but the reality was that the only way to achieve this was by indirectly precipitating his death. If Mr. P. had not been lucky enough to be on this medicine, he would have been forced to continue an existence that was excruciating and, to him, meaningless under current legal and professional constraints.

Most dying patients do not have a clearly defined route of exit. For those treated with comfort care, dying is usually at least tolerable, if not always peaceful. They may gradually slip into a coma, or develop a complication that precipitates a relatively benign final phase that is effectively managed using comfort-care principles. For others, death does not come easily in spite of a comfort-oriented approach. Some patients are forced to live on the edge of death for weeks or even months in semi-conscious states. They receive enough medication to keep them from being aware of their pain, but not so much that the medication will precipitate their death. Such patients must often make very difficult choices on a daily basis between pain and sedation. If feeding tubes or intravenous fluids are part of the treatment plan, patients can remain in this twilight zone indefinitely—a state where they are in too much pain to be awake, but have no immediate problem to precipitate death. For some people, such prolongation of dying might have a purpose; for others, it is meaningless and even cruel.

For a few patients, even those on hospice programs, the end can be agonizing and completely out of their control. Like Mr. P., some have progressive, untreatable medical problems that defy solution throughout the final course of their illness. Others are able to be maintained with relative comfort and dignity through most of their terminal illness, but the illness accelerates in its maliciousness toward the end. Some patients infected with human immunodeficiency virus (HIV) experience such ends. Not infrequently, near the end of a long and heroic struggle against the disease and its associated infections, the process begins irreversibly to attack their brain and eyesight. Many HIV-infected patients have become experts on their disease, both through extensive reading and through the experience of caring for others infected with the virus. For those who place extreme value on their physical and intellectual integrity, living out their final time with the progressive dementia associated with HIV can be far worse than death. "What dignity can be found dying demented, lying in my own feces, unaware of my surroundings?" they ask. The promise of comfort care is not overly soothing to some who have seen and may personally face this tragic end. A few choose an active end to their struggle through suicide, often acting in secret, isolated from their health-care providers and friends. Forcing such patients to choose between a "natural" death that they would find humiliating and secretly bypassing this end through suicide cannot be a part of humane care. The notion that such patients have to face this agonizing decision alone, often in secrecy, violates basic principles of humane care.

It is not only patients with HIV who force us to face the limits of a comfort-oriented approach. Another dramatic, at times excruciating lesson comes from the patients with lung or oral cancer who are dying of respiratory failure. These patients struggle to breathe, and are often continuously coughing and producing mucous in copious amounts. The morphine which we use to treat their pain and ease their struggle is helpful, though at times it may indirectly lessen the drive to breath and therefore inadvertently hasten death. This is a classic example of the "double effect," and is completely acceptable under principles of comfort care. When such patients eventually slip painlessly into a coma and die without an overwhelming struggle, we feel good about our job and about the efficacy of comfort care.

However, some patients with incurable respiratory problems have the opposite experience—they endure a panicked, suffocating struggle just prior to death that is very much like drowning. Dying of suffocation can be an excruciating ordeal for both the patient and the caregivers. The double effect suggests that one should give enough pain medicine to relieve suffering, but not an amount that intentionally precipitates death. Therefore, these agonizing ends are sometimes prolonged because of the unacceptability of directly intending death, even if death is the only escape from suffering. Some patients can live in an agonizing twilight between suffocation and death because of the ambiguity of our intentions. Attending doctors are only rarely at the bedside for these occurrences. More often it is nurses or family members who are operating under unclear directives with double meanings like "Keep him comfortable," or, "You can give her a little extra if she seems to need it." I am certain that some health-care providers and family members give patients enough medication to help their patient die under such circumstances, because most caring persons cannot continue to be present and watch such agony without responding.

The letters I received suggest that caregivers at the bedside feel abandoned by the medical profession under these circumstances. The profession appears to turn its back in these horrible moments in order to keep its intentions pure. Doctors cannot intentionally facilitate death, even if death is the only way to relieve a patient's overwhelming suffering. By maintaining this artificial distinction, our profession undermines the true intent of comfort care: to help people maintain dignity, control, and comfort all the way through the final phase of their illness until death. Because so many family members and friends have witnessed such very troubling deaths, it appears that this experience also undermines the public's trust that doctors will not abandon them if they are unfortunate enough to experience unbearable suffering prior to death.

The double effect captures a paradox in the care of the dying. It allows one to treat suffering with powerful measures that may hasten death. But intentionally accelerating death, even if it is the only escape from intolerable suffering, is not acceptable. The double effect does not acknowledge the fact that, for some patients, death is preferable to unremitting suffering. For other patients, it can also be preferable to the side effects of the treatments used to control pain and other symptoms. There is nothing selfish or improper about wanting a dignified, controlled death if one is incurably ill and has no other sensible options.

Many medical ethicists make a clear distinction between an active and passive role on the part of the physician in helping a patient to die. It is acceptable, for example, for a doctor to help a patient die by stopping a life-sustaining treatment, when requested to do so by the patient or if the treatment becomes medically futile. But it is not acceptable for a doctor actively to help a patient die who has an equal or greater amount of suffering, but who is not dependent on life-sustaining treatment that can be discontinued. Mr. P., the man with the brain tumor, was living a life without personal meaning, intolerable by almost anyone's standards, and surely by his own. Once we realized that one of his treatments was life-sustaining, we were able to offer him the option of stopping it with the purpose of "relieving his suffering." We knew that only death would provide this relief, but we could not outwardly show intent to produce death. Had Mr. P. not been on steroids, or had we not realized that they could be stopped, then he would have been forced to continue to live against his own wishes, with no hope of an exit other than a "natural" death under the current limitations of comfort care. Those who are dependent on life-sustaining treatments are the only patients who receive the medical right to choose death. No matter how excruciating and unrelenting their suffering, or how persuasive and rational their request, other patients are not allowed this possibility within current constraints. Patients who have the courage, physical strength, and means to act alone can still release themselves through suicide; but most are trapped to live out their sentence until death comes more passively and, at times, more agonizingly.

Patients who have kidney failure and are dependent on dialysis treatment are also given the option of choosing death. Dialysis is an example of a life-sustaining medical intervention with extraordinary benefits and substantial burdens. It can prolong the life of a patient whose kidneys have failed while they await a donor for potential transplantation. Others who are not candidates for transplantation can be maintained indefinitely with three half-days of dialysis each week. The treatments are time-consuming and have significant burdens in terms of repeated needle sticks, periods of nausea and weakness, and a host of potential physical, social, and financial complications. For most people, however, the burdens of dialysis, though considerable, are outweighed by the benefit of continued life.

Yet some patients on dialysis reach a point where the requirements of the treatment, combined with the suffering and limitations associated with their underlying illnesses, outweigh any meaning or enjoyment they can get out of life. It is generally accepted that the decision to discontinue dialysis can be rational—that a dialysis patient can reach a point where death is preferable to continued life with the accompanying burdens of treatment and illness. All attempts should be made to ensure that the patient's request to discontinue dialysis is not distorted by a treatable depression, or by unaddressed problems such as chronic pain. Despite these qualifications, many patients on dialysis die from having voluntarily discontinued treatment. The doctor plays an active role in ensuring that the patient has explored all other options, knows the consequences of his or her decision, and is not suffering from a distorting, treatable mental or physical illness. Yet, ethically, the doctor's role is passive in terms of helping the patient to die, since it is the patient who is discontinuing a life-sustaining treatment. In allowing the patient to stop dialysis, doctor and patient have come to acknowledge that there are no good options other than death. For the few days between the time dialysis is stopped and the patient dies, the patient is treated using comfort-care principles. The time frame is short, and patients can be heavily sedated in the interest of comfort while they await death.

In cases where the patient is dependent on a life-sustaining treatment, a doctor can ethically and legally assist the patient to achieve a relatively rapid, humane death. But there are frightening examples of the absurd lengths to which caring medical professionals must go to avoid directly assisting patients to die who are *not* dependent on such measures, in order to keep their intentions "pure." The following story was told to me informally by a colleague:

M R S. B.

Mrs. B. had had breast cancer for over ten years. For the first five years of her illness she lived fully, continuing her job as a school-teacher, being minimally bothered by her disease. But she unfortunately had an aggressive form of breast cancer, and the last five years of her life were mired by repeated hospitalizations, surgeries, hormonal therapies, chemotherapy, and radiation. At age sixty, she was nearing the end of a long ordeal—exhausted, weary, and losing hope of finding any solution that would have meaning for her. Her illness had forced her to give up teaching prematurely, and she was becoming more and more dependent on her three children and the health-care system. She had found the last six months completely empty, since she was bedbound from repeated fractures and forced to move to a nursing facility that also served as a hospice. There she made a few new friends and had some moments with her family that she viewed as tolerable. Yet, as she became weaker and could no longer read or even care for her basic bodily functions, she found her continued existence unbearable.

Mrs. B. clearly wanted to die. Her life had been stripped of all that was important to her. Death was the only thing she looked forward to. She no longer feared death, but was terrified about continuing to live under the current circumstances. She had nothing left to give.

As occurs all too often, death did not come in a timely way. Feeling trapped and desperate, Mrs. B. asked her personal physician for help. Her doctor cared deeply about Mrs. B. She knew from their shared, grueling experience, and from in-depth exploration of her reasoning, that Mrs. B.'s request was rational, and not distorted by depression. The doctor wanted to be helpful, but feared the potential professional and legal effects of providing active assistance. After getting permission from Mrs. B., the doctor decided to present the dilemma to the hospital ethics committee for guidance.

I am not privy to the deliberations of the ethics committee, but I *do know their recommendations. They suggested that the physician could actively treat Mrs. B.'s suffering by giving her enough morphine and sedation so that she became unconscious (therefore unaware of her suffering) and then letting her die by dehydration. This method, they felt, would be within the acceptable limits of comfort care, using the double effect to treat her suffering aggressively without intending death. Death would come passively, they presumably reasoned, through a more "natural" process. The committee suggested that providing active assistance by more forthrightly helping the patient to die would be outside of current professional and legal restraints, and therefore unadvisable.*

The doctor was very ambivalent and somewhat disturbed by the plan, but she reported the option to Mrs. B., who knew of the consultation. The doctor felt it was the only way she could respond to Mrs. B.'s request without taking a very large personal risk. (In fact, the risk of providing more "active" assistance had become even greater now that the patient's dilemma had been discussed in a relatively public forum.) Mrs. B. accepted the only option she had that would eventually ensure death. She subsequently said goodbye to her family and closest friends, and was put on an intravenous drip that contained morphine and a sedative, until she was unarousable. She remained in this state for ten days before dying, periodically attended by friends and family who found the experience deeply disturbing. Mrs. B.'s family had accepted her wish to die, but forcing her into a medically induced twilight zone so that she could then die of "natural causes" seemed macabre.

Mrs. B. was the second patient I heard of who was subjected to such a procedure. The solution seems humane on the surface, but feels more cruel and absurd as one thinks deeply about it. What was the intention of the treatment, or the committee, for that matter? What is our professional responsibility when death is clearly preferable to continued living and earnestly desired by the patient? If death is the only way the patient has to relieve suffering, then should it not be provided in the most humane manner possible when requested?

Many of the letters I received commented that we treat our pets better than we treat ourselves and our families. We would never allow our pets to be put into a coma so they could die of dehydration over a ten-day period, particularly if they could tell us that they were ready to die. It would be cruel to torture them prior to death. We love them too much to allow this to happen. Yet for human beings who have clearly articulated their wishes, our hands are tied—tied in part because we have difficulty accepting that for humans, death is sometimes the only escape from intolerable suffering. Allowing someone a peaceful, dignified death under such terrible circumstances can be a very sad, loving gift. Provided that all other options have been thoroughly explored and understood, and we are certain that this is what the patient wants, it may be the best of a very limited number of options one can offer under such dire circumstances.

SUICIDE IN THE TERMINALLY ILL

Some patients take matters into their own hands. Suicide itself is not illegal in the United States, providing one acts alone. Data about the frequency with which terminally ill patients kill themselves is fraught with reporting bias and uncertainty. The incidence of the problem is most certainly underestimated. Subtle forms of suicide, such as secret overdoses of medications by severely ill patients, are infrequently recorded on death certificates even if suspected by physicians. Raising the possibility of suicide by a physician or family member would almost certainly precipitate an investigation by the medical examiner. No matter how sick or near death the patient was before taking an overdose, or what the patient's or the family's wishes were, an autopsy and toxicology examination would be performed. If toxic levels of medications are found upon examination, the immediate cause of death would be ruled a suicide from a drug overdose.

Even if the patient was near death from an incurable illness, the determination of suicide as the immediate cause of death has many potentially adverse consequences. First, some patients' life insurance policies may be invalidated if there is a suicide exclusion. Depending on the patient's religion, she might not be allowed a traditional ceremony and burial. In addition to these tangible risks, there are many other more subtle aftereffects on the surviving family and friends. If they did not know about the reasons for the suicide, they may second-guess themselves for not doing more or for not recognizing the warning signs. They may take personal responsibility for an act that had nothing to do with them, and live forever with the worry that it might have been triggered by something that they said or did. If they were secret partners in the act, then they must either lie to the authorities to protect themselves from prosecution, or admit the truth and run the risk of being interrogated and potentially indicted as an accomplice. These factors and others probably result in a substantial underreporting of suicide in the severely ill.

The suicides that are reported tend to be outwardly visible. Self-inflicted gunshot, hanging, and asphyxiation all occur, though they may require more strength and energy than many terminally ill patients possess. If successful, patients who use these means to end their lives at least put an end (if gruesome) to their suffering. The victims more often are the families, who may both literally and figuratively have to pick up the pieces. Such ends leave permanent scars on the survivors, whose worries, self-doubt, and self-blame are intensified by the violence of these acts. Forcing patients who are terminally ill and suffering intolerably to choose between suicide and continued waiting for death in a life with no remaining meaning or dignity seems inhumane. Since the medical profession has been unwilling to acknowledge these problems, much less engage in an open discussion about possible solutions, it is no surprise that some patients are driven to such methods in despair and secrecy.

Published articles in the medical literature about suicide in the medically ill tend to treat it as an adverse outcome of unrecognized or untreated depression. Under such circumstances, it is correctly presented as an outcome to be prevented. I agree that depression is generally underrecognized and undertreated by primary-care physicians, but to think that the yearning for death experienced by some incurably ill, suffering patients can always be relieved by proper recognition and treatment of depression is a gross oversimplification. Distorted thinking arising from depression or other mental illness must be carefully looked into before an incurably ill patient's request for assisted death can be considered rational. Terminally ill patients tend to be sad, and the physical and emotional anguish that they face can precipitate a depression that might be treatable. A psychiatric consultation should be obtained if the physician is inexperienced in the diagnosis or treatment of depression, or if there is doubt about the presence of a treatable depression or irrational thinking. But doctors evaluating these patients need to be extremely realistic about the prospects that the patient has for the future. This is not a time for superficial assessments, or for unrealistic recommendations that are not directly negotiated with the dying patient. Rather, it is a time for in-depth exploration—checking the patient's understanding of his/her condition, experience of the present, views of the future, and knowledge of the treatment options available. Suicide that is triggered by a treatable depression, or by misconceptions about the reality of the patient's condition, should clearly be prevented. Requests for direct assistance in dying by people who are incurably ill, suffering severely, and show no mental distortion also need full exploration. Even though such explorations may be painful for the physician, the mandate to prevent such deaths when rationally requested is much less clear.

Many stories and letters I received reported unsuccessful suicide attempts, ranging from the patient's inability to take enough medication for an overdose to shooting themselves and surviving. Some patients were "saved" by their loving family or their physician, only to complete their sentence on this earth constantly monitored and experiencing constant resentment. Some of these acts were clearly desperate cries for help, whereas others were rational attempts to end suffering through death. If the suicide attempt led to a new recognition of something a doctor or family could do to help, or to a renewed sense of direction for the patient, then perhaps it could serve some purpose. If it led to more prevention and monitoring, with the caregivers or the patient still unable to improve the underlying circumstances that were intolerable to begin with, then such unsuccessful attempts add insult to injury.

Tragically, some terminally ill patients get weaker and weaker, to the point where suicide is no longer achievable on their own. For some individuals, the possibility of suicide is enough to keep them from feeling completely trapped. Others may kill themselves prematurely out of fear that they will lose the physical ability or the mental capacity to act in the future as their disease inevitably progresses. When disability increases to the point where suicide is no longer physically feasible, the dying person who prefers death to continued life becomes totally dependent on the goodwill and support of her physician and family. Not only does the patient lose the possibility of suicide as an escape, but if her competence comes into question, she may also lose control of other medical decisions, such as the use of intravenous hydration, which may prolong dying even further. Patients who lose competence need the advocacy of a fully informed Health Care Proxy, who knows the full scope of their wishes, to ensure that treatment will continue to be driven by the patient's own values, and not by those of the physician or the health-care institution. Choosing death, even passively, can become more difficult as one gets weaker and closer to the end.

I received many stories that chronicle heroic attempts to respond to dying patients who were in desperate need of an escape from their struggle with illness and dying. I have selected just one that was told to me by a woman who has been my patient for over fourteen years. Although a close relationship emanated from our work together over that time, I did not know until recently that she was a long-standing member of the Hemlock Society. As with many of my patients, reading my article about this forbidden topic opened up conversations that might otherwise have been unsafe to talk about. By sharing their secrets, my patients have acknowledged a reality that is more pervasive than I originally imagined. In exploring this frightening reality, we can each hope for something better when our own time comes.

B I L L

Bill was a physically fit, energetic man in his mid-seventies who still worked part time when he wasn't playing tennis or golf. He lived life fully, and was a joy to be with because of his thoughtfulness, sensitivity, and wit. His first encounter with a serious illness came when he suddenly lost the vision in the center of both of his eyes from the disease called macular degeneration. He became legally blind, and was unable to read, drive, or enjoy sports that required fine hand-eye coordination. Though he was devastated by this loss, he began to adjust and develop new skills to get around his deficit.

Several months later Bill was found to have cancer in his throat. Because the cancer had already spread to the lymph glands in his neck, Bill was not a candidate for operative treatment. Instead, he was offered treatment with radiation, which he was told had a good chance to control the disease. To take advantage of this chance, he would have to tolerate a sore mouth, difficulty swallowing, and perhaps some trouble hearing in the short run. With little hesitation or questioning, he began radiation treatment.

The reality of the radiation treatment was unfortunately harder than he imagined. He permanently lost most of his hearing, and could not swallow any solid foods. Though the tumor shrank, the hearing loss and the inability to eat solid foods persisted. He adjusted as well as he could to these severe losses, though his energy and joy of life never fully returned.

Over the subsequent eighteen months, Bill progressively lost weight. He had constant headaches and walking even short distances left him exhausted. His cancer began to rapidly grow, and he had difficulty even swallowing liquids. It had also spread to his sinuses and his brain—the drainage from his nose was so severe that he had to wear a pad to keep himself dry. Bill found this drainage from his nose and mouth to be humiliating, a constant outward reminder of his physical degradation. This once active, joyful, very proud man was now legally blind, severely hearing-impaired, constantly draining copious quantities of mucous from his nose, and unable to swallow most of his own secretions. After two years of progressive loss and misery, it could only get worse.

My patient was a retired nurse and a former hospice worker, as well as a Hemlock Society member. As a friend of the family with special knowledge and experience, she was called on for advice because of Bill's rapidly deteriorating condition. Bill's wife confided, with tears streaming down her face, that he was now actively thinking about committing suicide. My patient was asked if she would talk to Bill, and she consented. Bill's first words were, "I suppose you're going to try to talk me out of it, too." When she replied that she would not, Bill spoke openly of his anguish and helplessness, and about how he was only comforted by the potential release that would come with death. He now dreaded the process of dying much more than death itself, and he could no longer stand the indignity that continuing to live required. He talked at length about his love for his wife and about the unbearable frustration of being a burden for so long.

After several daily visits with Bill and his wife, there was no doubt in my patient's mind that Bill would take his life with or without anyone's approval. He never faltered in his belief that it was his only realistic option. Bill's wife gradually came to accept his decision, though she felt equally overwhelmed by his dying and by his continued living under current circumstances. When they began to discuss methods, Bill brought out a shotgun and discussed how he intended to use it. They also explored using an overdose of medications as recommended by the Hemlock Society. They discovered that Bill probably had enough potentially lethal medication for the suicide, provided he could swallow it all, and provided that someone would assist with the plastic bag if the overdose was insufficient (this is a backup measure described in the Hemlock Society literature). My patient's understanding and compassion for Bill now superseded her concern about her own legal liability should her role in his suicide be discovered. She was committed to being with Bill and his wife until the end, no matter where it took them.

A plan was made for Bill to take the overdose on his own the next day. My patient would assist with the plastic bag only if necessary. Elaborate arrangements were made for notifying the authorities, and what to report. Once Bill was dead, they would remove the bag and call the doctor to report that Bill was found dead of "natural causes." My patient went home that night uncertain what the next day would bring, but certain that Bill believed death was his best choice. She left Bill and his wife in a tearful embrace.

When my patient returned the next day, Bill told her that after deliberating all night, he had decided not to involve her in his death. He was worried about the legal vulnerability that she and his wife might incur if their assistance were discovered. Despite my patient's *protestations that she was willing to take this risk, he refused to change his mind, saying "I love you too much to risk your future." After a long, wide-ranging conversation, Bill excused himself to go to the bathroom. Within minutes there was a loud gunshot. Bill had shot himself through the head. Bill's wife and my patient ran in knowing what he had done, but not knowing what they would find. They found Bill gruesomely wounded, half dead and half alive.*

An ambulance and the police arrived, and took Bill to the hospital at high speed with sirens wailing. Bill's wife was completely numb, unable to think clearly or to speak. My patient felt impotent, enraged, and overwhelmed. They remained behind not knowing what to do as the ambulance crew whisked Bill away. After Bill was evaluated and resuscitated in the Emergency Department, it was evident that he was fatally wounded. A doctor called the home to inform the family that they might not be able to save him. Upon hearing, "Please don't try—he's suffered enough," the doctor responded, "I'll give him something for his pain and try to keep him comfortable."

Bill died three hours later.

Bill's wife will probably never recover, or forgive herself.

My patient will never forget the experience, and is more frightened than ever about the potential for unremitting end-of-life suffering.

Chapter 6

DEFINING MOMENTS

Compassion and Conflicting Responsibilities

Patients who have incurable illnesses that finally make living intolerable have few, if any, choices. The superficial solutions suggested by most medical professionals provide little solace or hope. They must face the consequences of continued living, no matter how difficult or unendurable. Some of these patients begin to look upon death not as an enemy but as the only escape from an unacceptable reality. A few who are physically and emotionally strong enough, and have access to and knowledge about means, begin seriously to consider the possibility of suicide. Finding a physician who can address this option with an open mind can often be very liberating for such a patient. The possibility of a controlled death can sometimes paradoxically free a dying person to choose to live more fully, rather than feeling trapped with no options at all.

One young man with early asymptomatic human immunodeficiency virus (HIV), who had nursed several friends who died of acquired immunodeficiency syndrome (AIDS), became preoccupied with the possibility that he would suffer needlessly in the future. He gradually obtained enough medicine to kill himself, just in case the need arose. He kept his "stash" in a blue sock, secure in the knowledge that an exit was possible in the future should he need one. This "stash" was known about and quietly accepted by all those who knew and cared for him. Years later, when he developed AIDS and progressively lost his health and independence, he surprised his family and friends by not taking his own life. However, he took his sock with him wherever he went for the last months, a symbol of his remaining freedom, defiance, and personal choice. After an excruciating six months of hospitalization, weight loss, invasive procedures, and loss of independence, he died quietly at home, sedated with a morphine drip, being treated under well-accepted principles of comfort care—his sock next to him under his pillow. He never explicitly asked others for help in dying, but always kept the option within reach.

Physicians, families, and close friends who care deeply about patients enduring end-of-life suffering are sometimes faced with a difficult dilemma. If the symptoms and suffering are relentless, each caretaker searches his or her conscience, knowledge, and creativity to be helpful. The principles of comfort care usually provide effective guidance. Applied broadly, caring persons can use such principles to help find solutions that can make most patients' situations tolerable, if not always comfortable. But what happens in the rare but heartbreaking circumstances when a loved one continues to experience life as unbearable and meaningless? What if they accurately perceive death as the only escape, and are adamant about choosing death sooner rather than later?

Many patients faced with the prospect of dying and the possibility of extreme suffering along the way experience thoughts or feelings about wanting to die. They have a clear vision of a future devoid of meaning or hope of recovery. Openly acknowledging and exploring these thoughts and feelings is a large step forward—by validating the patient's feelings of anguish and hopelessness, at least the patient is not left alone with them. But some dying people challenge us further. They may see no acceptable options for continued living, and want to die now rather than later. In their eyes, nothing further can be gained by continued living. Unfortunately, much more can be lost.

PUBLICIZED CASES

One of the reasons I chose to publish the article about my experience with Diane and her family was because the previous cases in the medical literature were relatively easy for medical ethicists, physicians, and institutions to dismiss. They lacked sufficient safeguards, and the physicians' actions seemed arbitrary and ill-considered. They seemed to take the emphasis away from the complex, emotionally wrenching dilemma faced by these patients and their families, and to focus attention instead on the physicians' flaws in thinking and methodology.

One anonymously published case entitled "It's Over, Debbie" was printed in the prestigious *Journal of the American Medical Association*. It describes a medical resident giving an overdose of morphine to a severely ill cancer patient who appeared near death, and who had given the ambiguous directive: "Let's get this over with." This report was criticized extensively because the resident was exhausted from being on call and had no prior knowledge of the patient or her condition. It was unclear whose misery—the resident's or the patient's—was ultimately being relieved. The resident had no way of understanding the full meaning of Debbie's plea for help. It was also unclear from the dose of morphine and the ambiguous language used in the article whether his intent was to relieve suffering or to produce death. Did death come inadvertently through the "double effect," or was it his primary intention? Nonetheless, the discussion that followed focused almost entirely on the "inappropriate" actions of the physician, and the danger of physicians becoming involved in such activities. The agonizing experience of the patient, and the potential legitimacy of her request, if properly understood, remained relatively unacknowledged and unexplored.

Several other publicized cases involve Dr. Jack Kevorkian and his now infamous "suicide machine." His provocative, alarming acts have focused national attention on the choices about death that doctors offer to patients who are incurably ill. Through his extreme actions, Dr. Kevorkian has forced medical ethicists and physicians to think more carefully about the rights and restrictions regarding a potential role in assisting the death of severely suffering patients. He has also deeply frightened us by the ease with which he helps patients to die, and by his apparent lack of doubt, uncertainty, or careful analysis of his patients and their problems. The debate generated by Dr. Kevorkian has focused primarily on him as a person, and on the absence of safeguards and the potential for abuse in his methods.

Many serious and legitimate concerns have been raised about Dr. Kevorkian and his actions. (1) He is a retired pathologist and not a clinician. He therefore does not have the knowledge and experience to ensure that all alternative medical approaches to achieving patient comfort have been exhausted, or that the patient's request for death is not distorted by depression. (2) He has been willing to act without a deep or long-standing relationship with the patient, and therefore may not have the emotional investment in his patient's well-being that should underlie such a profound decision to help. He has shown little interest in working with or learning from dying patients who are finding alternatives to suicide. (3) He had not thoroughly reviewed all available information about the irreversibility of each patient's illness, nor the extent to which comfort measures had been tried and failed. (4) He has assisted patients whose medical conditions have potential for considerable ambiguity and uncertainty, even for experts. The initial patient he assisted, Janet Adkins, had "early Alzheimer's disease." A later patient had an "ill defined uterine condition." (5) He has used these deaths to gain publicity to promote his own unusual ideas and approach to death. He appears more interested in challenging society and the medical profession than in engaging with individual dying patients in their struggle to find their own path.

The lack of rigor and safeguards in Dr. Kevorkian's methods has been unanimously criticized—and rightly so, in my estimation. His license to practice medicine has been revoked by the state of Michigan. In the fall of 1991 he was indicted for murder, but was subsequently not convicted in part because Michigan has no laws prohibiting assisted suicide. Despite the disapproval in almost all professional and legal circles, many among the general public support Dr. Kevorkian's actions. My belief is that his supporters are applauding his affirmation of individuals' need for more choice under such circumstances, his challenge to the medical profession which they see as selfishly avoiding the issue, and his willingness to take risks and offer provocative alternatives to current approaches. If we are frightened by Dr. Kevorkian's methods, we should begin to ask ourselves how the medical profession can be found so lacking that a superficial, bizarre approach to death can appeal strongly to the general public.

FINAL EXIT

If this weren't worrisome enough to those of us who are advocates for increased options in the humane care of the dying, we needed only look to the top of the self-help section of *The New York Times* best-seller list throughout a large portion of 1991.

There we found *Final Exit,* a "how-to" book about suicide for terminally ill persons written by Derek Humphry, the founder of the Hemlock Society. The public's intense interest in *Final Exit* should make each of us in the medical community wonder how we could be leaving our patients so desperately insecure. The book directly challenges traditional medical prohibitions about assisted suicide and euthanasia. Without full regard for the potential consequences, the book also presents detailed, explicit suicide methods for anyone's use.

In *Final Exit,* Humphry openly and nonjudgmentally presents the option of "self-deliverance," or assisted suicide, for terminally ill persons, based on anecdotal information accumulated through ten years of experience with the Hemlock Society, including personally assisting in three suicides within his own family. The techniques offered are explicit, including lethal doses of prescription medications, and the rationale for the plastic bag, which is a trademark of a Hemlock Society suicide. Although the discussion of pharmacokinetics and medication management is at times naive, most of the drug information appears accurate, practical, and potentially helpful to those few terminally ill persons who have no other way out. It is also a provocative political challenge to those who wish to minimize or ignore the complex dilemma posed by severe suffering and loss of personal dignity prior to death.

However, there are no guarantees and safeguards that this information will not be used by people with mental illnesses like depression that can transiently distort judgment, or by terminally ill persons who are experiencing passing moments of despondency. Easy access to such practical information about suicide can be dangerous. Yet our current public policy prohibits direct professional participation in these matters, even under the clearest and most excruciating of circumstances. It therefore forces some terminally ill persons to continue suffering against their will or to naively choose a method of suicide that may be ineffective or even violent. Humphry argues persuasively that doctors could humanely oversee this process because of their preexisting relationship with the patient, their ability to assess the patient's clinical prognosis and mental status, and their knowledge about and access to effective methods. Current laws create a paradox by prohibiting physician participation under any circumstances, but allowing explicit information about suicide methods to flow through the impersonal, uncontrolled, and potentially dangerous format of a book. Humphry and his colleagues at the Hemlock Society force us to face the consequences of this paradox. In the wrong hands, the consequences are both tragic and dangerous.

The mixture of extreme oversimplification with accurate depiction gives *Final Exit* an unsettling quality for those who support a thoughtful, conservative exploration of physician-assisted suicide. It suggests that physicians are currently reluctant because of the "stigma" of potentially prescribing lethal medications to emotionally ill persons instead of caring about protecting the sanctity of each individual's life. It advocates lying to doctors about insomnia to obtain lethal drugs when previous requests have not been successful, rather than continuing direct negotiation and exploration. To avoid the undermining effects of such deception on a relationship based on mutual trust, physicians must acknowledge their power over patients as controllers of a nonviolent escape from severe suffering. Such power cannot be wielded arbitrarily without in-depth understanding of the consequences.

As a guide for those with a terminal illness who are exploring the option of suicide, there are significant flaws in *Final Exit*. The complex thinking and feeling processes one goes through in deciding to end one's life are underdeveloped in the book. To minimize the struggle, trivialize its complexity, and discount the rich uniqueness of each individual's experience is to dehumanize the process of dying. The personal responsibility, conflict, and angst of the assisters is also grossly underestimated. To suggest that there are no long-term potential adverse emotional consequences for those who assist in these secret suicides is naive and misleading. Though suicide can in fact be rational, this does not imply that it is devoid of feelings of doubt, guilt, grief, and anger for the survivors. Some who assist are permanently changed by the experience and need extensive counseling to unravel their complex, conflicting feelings about responsibility.

Unfortunately, *Final Exit* also deemphasizes the fact that comfort care can adequately and humanely relieve suffering and pain most of the time for incurably ill persons. Instead of enthusiastically offering comfort care to all patients who don't want life-prolonging treatment, an "either-or" decision is implied between assisted suicide and comfort care. Since comfort care is effective most of the time, assisted suicide should only be considered as a last resort when such care fails adequately to relieve suffering, or the personal costs of the struggle to continue living become too high. The naive reader of *Final Exit* who is suffering from an incurable illness might form the impression that there are not effective alternatives to suicide—alternatives that should be fully explored before this extreme option is seriously considered.

The success of Humphry's book attests to the widespread fear of abandonment that persons have should they be unfortunate enough to enter into a state of unrelenting terminal suffering. This fear is not going to be relieved until the medical profession acknowledges that severe end-of-life suffering sometimes exists despite adequate efforts to provide comfort care, and that patients in this heartbreaking condition should be given as much control and choice as possible. This requires a serious reexamination of traditional medical practices. It is not enough to say that what we need is more physician training in comfort care, or that this is an area that physicians should avoid because it violates traditional medical values. If we are going to continue to prohibit doctors from assisting patients who see death as the only answer to their tragic state of terminal suffering, then we need to provide guidance to doctors and information to patients about what options they do have. *Final Exit*'s success suggests that if the medical profession continues to turn its back, some members of the public will act on their own.

WITNESSES

How can we as caring, responsible professionals, family members, or friends respond to requests by gravely ill patients for help in dying with what little dignity remains to them? It is safe to say that thoughts about suicide and wishes about death are not infrequent in the terminally ill. How often those thoughts and feelings, once fully explored and understood, evolve into a persisting desire for death is much less certain. Indirect evidence of the scope of end-of-life suffering was brought home to me in the two thousand letters I received in response to my article about Diane. In many of these letters, experienced physicians as well as family members lamented their impotence despite extraordinary, comprehensively applied efforts to provide comfort care. Being a witness to unrelenting suffering, when there is no hope of recovery and no acceptable way to maintain dignity, has profound personal consequences. Repeated allusions to a "living nightmare," "complete humiliation," and "complete loss of dignity" were made by caregivers who will never forget or forgive themselves in spite of their heroic efforts to provide comfort. Allowing a person's death to be dominated by hopelessness, despair, unrelenting agitation, or unrelieved symptoms left permanent psychological and spiritual scars on the survivors: "I just prayed for his release. . . . It is hard for me to believe that a loving God or a caring profession would allow such suffering. . . . It is beyond words to see your beloved in such agony. . . . I will never forgive myself."

In my original article, I wondered how many family members

and doctors helped their "beloved" over the edge into death in the face of such severe suffering. The letters and stories that I received support the notion that many physicians and family members have secretly helped patients to die under exceptional circumstances. This correspondence focused largely on the intense personal experiences of the patients and caretakers who face these insoluble dilemmas where there are no good options. Data about the frequency of physician-assisted death are fraught with imprecisely worded questions that can be variably interpreted ("Have you ever helped a patient to die?") and biases in sampling because of the potential risk involved in responding honestly. These flawed data suggest that from 3 to 37 percent of physician respondents have "actively assisted" at least one of their patients to die. Since almost all practitioners who work with very ill patients periodically face this dilemma, this statistic is not at all surprising to me. Oncologists and physicians specializing in AIDS cannot possibly escape the question, but most primary-care physicians with large practices are also not immune. Responses to the dilemmas posed by these patients in the current uncertain professional and legal environment are varied and idiosyncratic, depending more on the values and willingness to take risks of the doctor than the patient.

In the letters and stories that I received, requests for assisted death—when they came in the context of an intimate relationship—became a self-defining moment for each person involved. Religion, law, and personal values of the caregivers often conflicted with the dying person's request. The mandate to ensure the patient's comfort and dignity, but not to intentionally hasten death, appeared impossible. Most of the writers had witnessed the patient's illness intimately and knew from direct experience that all acceptable alternatives had been tried. A patient's request for assisted death often seemed simultaneously legitimate, heartbreaking, and terrifying to the caregivers. Watching patients beg for assistance that did not come seemed cruel, adding a final humiliation to a process that was already grueling and undermining. For some caregivers, strongly held personal values dominated their decision making, often allowing the patient's request to be acceded to or denied with relative clarity and ease. For others, it triggered a self-defining struggle that challenged their personal values no matter how they responded.

DEFINING MOMENTS

Shortly after reading my article, a routinely scheduled patient of mine told me she had given her mother a lot of morphine when she was dying of cancer. I guessed she was concerned she might have unintentionally hastened her mother's death through the "double effect," and I supported her efforts to keep her mother comfortable, even if they had inadvertently shortened her life. She corrected my misunderstanding by letting me know that one night she kept giving her mother morphine until she died. Her mother wanted to join her husband, who had died the previous year. She had lost her independence, and was losing her clarity of thought when kept "comfortable" with the use of potent analgesics. Because she saw only further disability and loss of dignity in her future, she asked her daughter to help. Once my patient had assured herself that her mother's request was clear-minded and unambivalent, she was able to act decisively, without extensive second-guessing. She had witnessed her mother's slow, at times humiliating decline, and knew of her long-standing values and wishes against lingering further with a terminal illness. Afterwards my patient appeared to have a clear conscience. She perceived it to be an act of love that spared her mother unnecessary and unwanted suffering, and involved little conflict within either her own or her mother's personal values.

Another of my patients spontaneously told me that I was the most courageous man he had ever known. Though I was both flattered and embarrassed by the compliment, it raised my curiosity as to why this story seemed so heroic to him. When this man's father was dying a horrible death from cancer many years earlier, he had repeatedly begged my patient to "put him out of his misery." Watching his father suffer for weeks on end with no relief was overwhelming. The man felt that his father's request was legitimate, and searched for some way to accommodate it. Unfortunately, he had no means to allow a quiet, dignified death that would go undetected by the legal authorities. He did have several guns, and his father, who was by then very weak, asked my patient to help him use the gun to kill himself. My patient was not a timid person, yet he, not surprisingly, could not bring himself to help his father in this way. After several more humiliating months, his father died in the hospital of "natural causes." My patient feels that he abandoned his father at the time in life when he most needed help. Though one might rightly argue that his father's request was unfair, in fact the father had nowhere else to turn. His own physician did not consider a request for death legitimate, and the father was too weak physically to take matters entirely into his own hands. My patient will always second-guess himself for not having the "courage" to respond to his father's request.

Another son—a doctor—told a similar story with a different outcome. His father, also a doctor, was dying from the relentless progression of widely metastatic lung cancer. The son and other family members altered their schedules and joined with members of a hospice team to provide twenty-four-hour care, which included regular around-the-clock use of narcotic analgesics for pain control. Though relatively free of pain, the father felt degraded by his physical deterioration, his inability to manage his personal hygiene, and his decreased mental clarity when taking medication. He began to talk regularly about wanting to die and escape this life, which he was finding more and more intolerable. One evening, in between doses of medicine, the father said to his son, "I want you to give me my shot, but I do not want to awaken again. I am now ready to join your mother." The father had helped his wife die comfortably in the past when she was suffering from widely metastatic cancer. The son made certain that he fully understood his father's request. After a long talk about the meaning of continued life and actively choosing death, the son administered a lethal dose of medication. He kept this act a secret even from his family for years—wondering if he had given in too easily or if he was totally correct in his decision. The uncertainty surrounding his "act of love" still haunts this son, though he feels certain he was carrying out his father's final wishes, and that comfort-care methods had been fully utilized and exhausted. Physicians and their families are relatively fortunate in that they have ready access to nonviolent means to ensure death should such tragic circumstances arise. Nonetheless, the secrecy surrounding the decision making and the act itself can have profoundly isolating and undermining effects on the survivors.

Many letters showed that otherwise healthy, competent persons fear the loss of control, helplessness, and prolonged dependence should they become irreversibly sick in the future. Some reported surreptitiously hoarding enough medicine to kill themselves should a future need arise. A few very ill patients reported "pseudo-conversations" with their physicians, whereby potentially lethal medicine was prescribed under the guise of pain relief or sleeplessness. Sometimes patients knowingly deceive their physicians, afraid to share their true intent for fear they will withhold the desired prescription. Others report multilayered transactions with both patient *and* doctor knowing the true intent of the prescription, but not explicitly talking about it: "Be careful, because if you take too much it could kill you."

Many letters came from members of the Hemlock Society, an organization devoted to advocacy for a patient's right to choose death when faced with an incurable illness, including the provision on request of specific "how-to" information about suicide. The Hemlock Society reportedly has 75 chapters, with 72,000 dues-paying members in the United States, attesting to the widespread fear of needless suffering at the end of a serious illness, and to the desire for some control over one's ultimate destiny. Those members who had found a lethal supply of medicine reported feeling more secure with the knowledge that death with dignity and personal control was possible, even though they hoped they would never need it. In my opinion, the conversations that result in these prescriptions are too serious and important to include any secrecy or deception. The stakes are too high, and the adverse effects of potential miscommunication too profound. Yet the legal and professional prohibitions against a doctor's direct participation in helping severely ill, suffering patients to die make honest, open communication risky—for many, forbiddingly so.

A woman with advanced cancer, having lost her independence with nothing to look forward to other than death, decided it was her time to die. Neither her doctor nor her husband was willing to address her wishes seriously; they insisted that she not think that way, or at least not talk about such matters. They cared deeply about her and wanted her to live as long as possible, no matter what the price. They were also intensely uncomfortable and unwilling to talk openly about the prospect of her impending death, or about how intolerable she found continued living. Over time, the patient saved up a lethal dose of medicine. Eventually, the woman attempted suicide by taking an overdose. She did not inform her husband or her physician in order to protect herself from their prohibitions and to protect them from future legal consequences. As she was becoming unconscious, her husband came home, panicked, and called an ambulance. Cardiopulmonary resuscitation was initiated, she was put on a breathing machine, her stomach was pumped, and she was admitted to a hospital intensive-care unit. There she was "saved" to go home and complete her sentence of an additional three months of comfort care, which she experienced with despair.

Because of her attempted suicide, this woman was evaluated by a psychiatrist who found her to be sad, but not depressed in any way that was reversible or distorting her perception of the reality of her illness. The physician's subsequent prescriptions for pain medicines were conservative, and tightly monitored. She received no sleeping pills in spite of troubling insomnia because her physician now felt that she could not be trusted with them. She never forgave her husband for subjecting her to this unwanted end, and he subsequently never forgave himself.

Many patients infected with HIV know only too well what the last phases of the illness can look like. It is difficult for an honest doctor to be reassuring to those suffering from a progressive loss of vision from cytomegalovirus infection, or from the severe wasting that begins to be associated with central nervous system deterioration. Some doctors working with HIV-infected patients quietly acknowledge the problem, and prescribe potentially lethal doses of medications upon request in a secret pact with their patients. Other doctors believe it is their duty to continue to fight for life no matter how severe the illness, and pressure their patients to continue life-prolonging treatments no matter how severe the patient's condition, while discounting and discouraging any talk about giving in to death. Many HIV-infected patients tragically wonder, when their time comes, whether they will be able to find a physician who will help them avoid this final devastating phase.

It is clear from the stories that some physicians actively help a few of their patients over the edge under special circumstances. Most physicians have kept their experiences private, except perhaps with their most trusted colleagues. Many letters from doctors confirmed an understanding that comfort and peace at the time of death are ideals to be sought, but included acknowledgment that the reality of dying—especially the last phases—is often much more complex and disturbing. Several doctors wrote of their dying patients' relief, comfort, and security when they prescribed requested barbiturates for sleep, but also for possible overdose in case their suffering became too intense or unrelenting. Not so subtle hints such as "You can take these pills to help you sleep, but if you take too many it would kill you" were reported. Some physicians reported that few of their patients who received such prescriptions actually used them to overdose. Those doctors whose patients had themselves been doctors wrote how relatively common secret suicide was for their colleagues who became severely ill. Physicians, it appears, have the luxury of not being dependent on the goodwill and common values of others in order to choose a nonviolent death.

Some doctors also wrote of giving clearly lethal doses of medication to patients who were suffering on the edge of death with no prospect of recovery. They felt that, under these excruciating circumstances, the intentions and the prohibitions within the "double effect" merged—that death was the only way to relieve their patients' suffering. Some were plagued with self-doubt, wondering if they went too far, or if they should have done more medically before giving in to a patient's request. Others worried that they had not been decisive enough, and that their patients may have suffered needlessly at the end because of their hesitancy. Often the secrecy surrounding the act was preoccupying and isolating. It is remarkable to me how telling one of these secret stories publicly has unleashed such a wealth of profound yet troubling human experience.

One particularly moving story was from a doctor who prescribed barbiturates to a patient with advanced AIDS to give him the security of an exit should he need it. Several hospitalizations later, with increasing disability, dependence, and death in his future, the patient decided it was time to call it quits. The patient decided to have a farewell party where he could say goodbye to his closest friends, and the doctor was invited. The patient lay on a hospital bed in his own living room, and his friends reminisced with him about shared experiences over the years. After saying their final goodbyes, the patient asked his doctor to stay on when everyone else left. The patient wanted to take the barbiturates he had saved for an overdose, but was too weak to feed them to himself. Faced with this moment of truth, the doctor helped his patient swallow the pills. The patient gradually went into a coma and died quietly in his physician's arms. Though the edges of the law and his own personal values were severely tested, this doctor found the courage, compassion, and conviction not to abandon his patient, nor to sentence him to weeks or months of potential unwanted suffering and dependency if he turned his back.

There is general agreement that one of our central missions as physicians is to use whatever personal and medical resources we have to relieve the symptoms and maintain the integrity of dying persons, even if such measures might inadvertently hasten death. Yet what are our responsibilities when death is the only way to end the suffering, and continued life requires continued disintegration of the dying person? What should we do in such tragic circumstances when those we love and care about request our help? As caregivers, each of us may have lines that we rarely cross and lines that we never cross in our efforts to fulfill our responsibilities. When a dying person's little remaining dignity is rapidly deteriorating, and she requests help in achieving a quiet, dignified death, some of our usual limits may shift. Whether we assist such a person to die on her own terms, or hold back because of religious, legal, societal, or personal values, the choice we make has a profound, long-lasting effect on both the sufferer and the caregiver.

Chapter 7

PUBLIC POLICY

*Exploring a Wider Range of Options
for the Dying*

Developing a public policy that can be responsive to the needs of patients who face these troubling dilemmas toward the end of their life, while simultaneously protecting them from being inadvertently abused by social and economic forces, will be difficult. The decision to move forward must depend on a careful comparison of the benefits and risks of liberalizing policy under carefully defined circumstances, versus maintaining the current blanket restrictions, with their inability to recognize patients with pressing, tragic needs.

TERMINOLOGY

The debate about physician-assisted death thus far has been clouded by imprecise, sometimes inflammatory use of language. The descriptive term "physician-assisted death" includes both physician-assisted suicide and voluntary active euthanasia. It emphasizes the physician's role as an assistant to an act initiated by the patient. Doctors "killing" patients is technically correct, but it incorrectly suggests a physician-driven act, and brings out uneasy visions of the Holocaust, in which a vicious abuse of physician power was used to systematically exterminate those who were deemed to be socially unworthy. Nothing could be further from the intent of those who favor a limited reconsideration of public policy in the areas of assisted suicide and voluntary active euthanasia. Physicians are reluctant partners in assisted dying, motivated by the compassion they feel toward suffering patients who request their help and have no good alternatives.

Suicide is defined as the intentional taking of one's own life, but its multilayered meaning emerges in a second definition which includes the self-destruction of one's own personal interests. In the medical literature, suicide is almost always viewed as an act of despair and self-destructiveness, the outgrowth of untreated depression and impaired rational thought. Suicide in that context is clearly something to be prevented, and physicians' appropriate role is to use all their resources, including enforced hospitalization if necessary, to help patients regain their will to live.

Suicide in the context of end-stage medical illness associated with irreversible suffering that can only end in death can have a different meaning. Many believe that suicide under such circumstances can be rational—it is hard to judge the wish for an end to intolerable suffering that can only end in death as irrational. Under such tragic circumstances, death can sometimes provide the only relief. The only question is, how much more one must endure until it comes. Yet, because patients with such severe medical conditions are usually sad if not clinically depressed, it can at times be difficult to determine whether emotional responses to their illnesses are distorting their decision making. If there is any question that depression or other mental illness is coloring the patient's judgment, then consultation by an experienced psychiatrist or psychologist is necessary to understand the full implications of an incurably ill patient's request for assisted death.

In "assisted suicide," a patient is still carrying out his own act, but he is indirectly helped by an "assistant." When the assistant is motivated by compassion for an incurably ill patient who clearly and repeatedly requests help, the act can be ethical and moral, if not legal. If the assistant is motivated by greed, or if there is uncertainty about the rationality or motivation behind the patient's request, then the act of assistance becomes immoral, unethical, as well as illegal. There is little case-based legal definition for what kind of compassionate "assistance" might be considered illegal. For example, a physician might prescribe a potentially lethal supply of medication, along with information about what dose would be lethal and what dose would be medicinal. There the physician's intention could be explicitly to give the patient the option of taking her own life, or it might be more ambiguous. ("Don't take all of them or it could kill you.") Do we want dying patients to have such information and choice, or should we perhaps protect them from themselves by depriving them of potent medication that might be used to take their own lives? It is very difficult to prosecute doctors successfully in the face of such ambiguity, especially if they are clearly motivated by compassion for their terminally ill patients rather than self-interest.

Many dying patients often have potentially lethal doses of medication at home that are being used to treat their symptoms. To withhold such medicine because of an abstract fear about suicide would be immoral, and in violation of fundamental principles of comfort care. Unfortunately, some physicians continue to under-medicate potentially treatable symptoms of dying patients, in part out of vague fears about patient suicide, but probably as significantly by their fear of legal or professional investigation should their patient take an overdose. If the patient is suffering from a reversible depression that is distorting her judgment, then caution and conservatism must be exercised until the distortion is resolved. Yet undertreating a dying patient's symptoms because of unsubstantiated fears about liability is unfortunately quite legal, though clearly unethical and immoral.

There are laws in thirty-six states, including New York State where I practice, prohibiting assisted suicide. The intent of these laws is presumably to prohibit persons from promoting a suicide for malicious intent, for example, by giving a loaded gun to a rich relative who is experiencing transient depression. No physician or family member has ever been convicted of assisting in the suicide of a severely ill patient with intractable suffering. Such acts appear to be looked upon by juries as acts of compassion not intended to be covered by the law. Yet the laws exist, and the threat of professional or legal repercussions is severe enough to prohibit many doctors from assisting their patients even when they consider the patients' requests rational and compelling. These laws perpetuate and exaggerate the power differences between vulnerable patients and their physicians, and put patients' fates more than ever at the discretion of their physicians.

In physician-assisted suicide, the patient commits the final act herself. The physician's participation is indirect, and there can always be a reasonable doubt about the intention as long as the prescribed drug has other medicinal uses. My patient, Diane, felt she had to be alone at her death in order to maintain this legal ambiguity, and to protect her family and me should her act ever be discovered. No one should *have* to be alone at death to protect anyone. Ironically and tragically, my innocence in the eyes of the grand jury, which investigated my involvement with Diane in response to the article, was determined in no small measure by the fact that I was not present at her death. Laws that indirectly promote loneliness and abandonment at death should be carefully reconsidered to ensure that they don't have the unintended effect of further isolating and disempowering rather than protecting the dying person.

Euthanasia is defined as the act of painlessly putting to death a person who is suffering from an incurable, painful disease or condition. Its definition suggests a quiet and easy death—a "good death," to be contrasted with some of the "bad death" stories told in earlier chapters. Euthanasia is equated by some with "mercy killing," and its mention raises worries about involuntary killing and progressive disregard for human life. For others, the images of a painless escape from extreme suffering into death offer the promise of more compassionate and humane options for the dying. Unlike assisted suicide, where the legal implications have yet to be fully clarified, euthanasia is illegal in all states in the United States and likely to be vigorously prosecuted. It is also illegal in all other countries, though in the Netherlands it is explicitly left unprosecuted provided that specific guidelines are met.

Several distinctions are of critical importance in a serious discussion about euthanasia. The first is "voluntary" versus "involuntary," and the second is "active" versus "passive." "Voluntary" euthanasia means that the act of putting the person to death is the end result of the person's own free will. Consideration of voluntary euthanasia as an option, and the request for its use, must emanate from the patient *and no one else.* The patient's rational thought processes must not be distorted by depression or other sources of cognitive impairment. Unlike assisted suicide, where the physician provides the means for the patient to subsequently use, in euthanasia the physician is the direct agent of death. Although voluntary euthanasia can potentially be as humane and morally justifiable as assisted suicide, it puts the physician in a very powerful position. Many physicians and policy makers feel great trepidation because of the potential for abuse (e.g., physician-initiated euthanasia on incompetent patients or in ambiguous situations) or error (e.g., the patient changing her mind at the last minute).

"Involuntary" euthanasia means that the person is put to death without explicitly requesting it. Although this could be an act motivated by compassion for a severely suffering, incompetent patient, there is too much subjectivity and personal variation in the definition of "suffering" to condone such "acts of mercy." Involuntary euthanasia could also be used for completely immoral purposes—for example, on incompetent or even competent persons as an act of eugenics and social manipulation. Such abuses were witnessed in Nazi Germany, as we should never forget. Involuntary euthanasia, even when compassionately motivated, should remain criminal, and should be vigorously prosecuted and prohibited.

Involuntary euthanasia is a fundamentally different act both morally and ethically from responding to a voluntary request for euthanasia by a competent patient who has no escape from his suffering other than death. Voluntary euthanasia is an area worthy of our serious consideration, since it would allow patients who have exhausted all other reasonable options to choose death rather than continue suffering. Involuntary euthanasia, even when compassionately motivated, is extremely dangerous ground because of the inevitable subjectivity and personal variation of human suffering, and because of the potential for social abuse when one starts making such profound decisions on behalf of other persons who cannot express their own wishes. Perhaps fully competent suffering persons should be given the possibility of making such decisions for themselves; but under no circumstances should we allow such decisions to be made on behalf of those who are incompetent.

The distinction between "active" and "passive" euthanasia rests upon the assumption that it is ethically permissible for physicians to withhold or withdraw life-sustaining medical treatment at the patient's request, and let the patient die passively of "natural causes." Such "passive" euthanasia is based on the fundamental ethical principle that informed, autonomous patients have the right to refuse any and all medical treatments, no matter what the consequences. Yet, under circumstances of identical or even greater suffering where no life-sustaining treatment is being used, current law forbids the physician to take direct action designed to achieve the same end—even if it is rationally requested by the patient and would result in a more humane death. Passive euthanasia, along with the double effect of narcotic pain medicine, probably accounts for the vast majority of the estimated six thousand planned deaths in United States hospitals each day. How many times lines are secretly crossed and distinctions blurred in the care of these dying patients is simply not known.

Some ethicists believe that there is a fundamentally important distinction between active and passive euthanasia. Death is the intended outcome in both circumstances, but the physicians' actions are directly causal in active euthanasia, whereas it is the physicians' "inaction" in passive euthanasia that allows the patient to die of "natural causes." By maintaining this distinction, the medical profession allegedly remains untainted by becoming an agent of death. Yet, in the cloudy world of patient care, these distinctions can become more illusory than real, and our attempts to remain ethically pure sometimes extract a considerable price from dying persons who have little left to give. The intent of both active and passive euthanasia is to finally allow the patient with no other good options to die in the most humane way possible.

One does not need to have a great deal of medical experience to find an example of passive euthanasia resulting in a very difficult death from "natural causes." Take for example a patient with end-stage, metastatic lung cancer who is near death from respiratory failure. He has tried to prolong his life through chemotherapy and radiation, but is now losing weight, extremely short of breath, and nearing the end of the road. He has elected to forgo cardiopulmonary resuscitation and mechanical ventilation (breathing machine) and knows that his death is inevitable. In fact, he has even begun to look forward to death as an escape from his life, which now feels completely empty, devoid of future or hope. So far, most physicians and ethicists would be comfortable with this example of passive euthanasia, allowing the person to die "naturally" of respiratory failure rather than prolonging his death by putting him on a mechanical ventilator.

Yet suppose that this patient has an overwhelming fear of suffocation, and wants to go to sleep quickly and not wake up, rather than continuing the agony of gradual suffocation for days or even weeks prior to his inevitable death. His request is confirmed to be rational, and his family agrees that he should be spared this final struggle if at all possible. Since there is no life-sustaining treatment to discontinue, passive euthanasia does not provide help or guidance at this point. According to comfort care principles, his shortness of breath can be treated with narcotics in doses intended to limit the feelings of discomfort, but not to intentionally produce death. His shortness of breath and feelings of extreme anxiety are therefore treated with an infusion of morphine until he falls asleep and appears relaxed. Yet periodically he awakens, thrashing and screaming from a terrifying feeling of suffocation. His morphine dose is appropriately increased to the point that he is relaxed enough to again lose consciousness, and no further. Unfortunately, a primitive drive to continue breathing sustains him whenever he drifts off into sleep. He alternates between periods of extreme agitation and a medicated sleep on the edge of death, where he lingers for over a week on gradually increasing doses of morphine before finally succumbing. Anyone who has witnessed such "natural deaths" cannot help but be troubled by their nightmarish quality.

The option of a physician-assisted death, whether by assisted suicide or active voluntary euthanasia, would allow patients such as this an escape from meaningless torment prior to death. When death is the only way to relieve suffering, and inevitable regardless, why not allow it to come in the most humane and dignified way possible? Why is it considered ethical to die of "natural causes" after a long heroic fight against illness filled with "unnatural" life-prolonging medical interventions, and unethical to allow patients to take charge at the end of a long illness and choose to die painlessly and quickly? Most of us hope to be fortunate enough to experience a "good death" when we have to die, and to be spared an agonizing ordeal at the very end. Many of us hope that if we do end up in such unfortunate circumstances, we can find a physician who will help us creatively explore all possibilities, including facilitating a relatively quick and painless death. Hopefully we will never need it, but the possibility would be very reassuring.

THE NETHERLANDS

Would legalizing physician-assisted death allow more of us to die with dignity; or, as many allege, would it be an expression of our progressive devaluation of human life? Perhaps the experience in the Netherlands, where active voluntary euthanasia (though it remains technically a crime) has been openly practiced for ten years, can provide some guidance. Euthanasia has considerable public and professional support in the Netherlands, and the freedom from prosecution for participating physicians is supported by a substantial body of case law.

In 1984, the Dutch Medical Association established guidelines for performing euthanasia which were supported by a governmental commission the subsequent year. Although the commission recommended formal legalization, this has not occurred for complex political reasons. Physicians report feeling uncomfortable about the apparent contradiction between public policy and the law, but many are apparently willing to assist a few of their patients with terminal suffering to die in spite of the ambiguity. There has been much speculation and anecdotal reporting about the prevalence of euthanasia in the Netherlands, and concern about potential "slippage" from voluntary to involuntary practices.

Four criteria must be met in the Netherlands for euthanasia to be performed:

1. The patient must have an incurable disease and be suffering intolerably, with no prospect of relief. There is no requirement that the patient be imminently terminal, and no prognostic time limit where death is anticipated without euthanasia.
2. The request for assisted death must be initiated by the patient, uncoerced, and repeated over a reasonable period of time. The request must also be well documented. The intent of this requirement is to keep euthanasia from being performed on a person who has a transient wish for death stemming from momentary feelings of desperation, depression, or anger, but who would later change his mind.
3. The patient must be competent, and fully informed about his illness, the treatment options, and the prognosis. Requirements 2 and 3 ensure that euthanasia is voluntary, and restricted to fully competent persons. These guidelines clearly exclude incompetent patients, even when their suffering appears extreme. Advance directives requesting euthanasia are not recognized.
4. Euthanasia must be performed by a physician only after the previous criteria have been verified by a second physician not involved in the patient's care. The method used is usually a dose of barbiturates in order to induce sedation, followed by a lethal injection of curare. The guidelines clearly call for reporting all cases of euthanasia, yet many doctors still record that the patient died of "natural causes" on the death certificate. They cite their fear about the ambiguity between accepted policy and the law as their motivation for keeping the act secret, though critics believe that it may not be reported because the criteria are not being fully followed.

It is clear from the guidelines outlined above that only voluntary euthanasia would meet all four criteria. Still, there has been considerable speculation and reporting of a possible covert practice of compassionately motivated but involuntary euthanasia.* The government of the Netherlands recently completed a comprehensive survey of the practice of euthanasia, which begins to address some of these concerns in a more objective way.† They interviewed 405 Dutch physicians who provided primary medical care for 89 percent of the patients who died in the Netherlands in the year of the study. They also retrospectively reviewed 7,000 deaths, and achieved a 76 percent response rate for the questionnaires they sent to physicians to review these deaths. Subsequently, the deaths of 2,250 patients cared for by the original group of 405 physicians were prospectively reviewed over the ensuing six months. All responding doctors were interviewed in confidence and granted legal immunity for the information reported.

The researchers looked for three kinds of assisted death: (1) nontreatment decisions which indirectly hastened death, analogous to passive euthanasia; (2) alleviation of pain or symptoms with high doses of narcotics, comparable to the potential "double effect" of medications; and (3) active euthanasia and assisted suicide. As we have seen, passive euthanasia and the double effect of narcotics are currently accepted parts of terminal care in the Netherlands as in the United States, so the open practice of active euthanasia and assisted suicide is the new ground.

Summarizing data from the confidential interviews and the retrospective and prospective review of deaths, 35 percent of deaths in the Netherlands could be accounted for by nontreatment deci-

*See C. F. Gomez, *Regulating Death: Euthanasia and the Case of the Netherlands* (New York: Free Press, 1991).

†See P. J. van der Maas, et al., in *The Lancet,* 1991;338:669–74 for an English summary.

sions (passive euthanasia) and the double effect of narcotics. Only 1.8 percent of deaths were attributed to active euthanasia, and 0.3 percent were the result of physician-assisted suicide (1,900 deaths overall). In 0.8 percent of deaths, drugs were administered with the explicit intent of shortening the patient's life without meeting all four criteria. In half of these cases, the patient had previously expressed a wish for euthanasia should his or her suffering become extreme, but lost competence in the final moments of disease. The authors report that most of the other "exceptions" were for "unbearable" suffering, and they contend that these deaths were closer to the double effect of narcotic pain medicine intended to relieve suffering than active euthanasia. Not enough data is presented about these worrisome "exceptions" to accurately judge whether they represent abuses, or simply reflect the edges of an effective, humane practice. Hopefully, as the details of this complex study are translated, they can be more fully examined and compared with exceptional (largely secret) cases in the United States where the double effect is stretched to address the agonizing dilemmas posed by our own suffering patients.

The study provided a considerable amount of useful information about the processes of requesting and receiving euthanasia in the Netherlands. Uncontrolled physical pain was the exclusive reason given for requesting euthanasia for only 5 percent of those requesting. More commonly it was a complex mixture of "loss of dignity" (57%), "pain" (46%), "unworthy dying" (46%), "being dependent on others" (33%), and feeling "tired of living" (23%). While 25,000 patients per year seek reassurance from their doctors that they will provide euthanasia if their suffering becomes unbearable, only 9,000 patients made an actual request, of which 3,000 were agreed to by the physician. Of these 3,000 agreed to, 1,900 were carried out. Fourteen percent of requests were refused on psychiatric grounds. There averaged less than one request per physician per year (0.25 to 0.8) for the general practitioners who comprised the bulk of the respondents. Most reported being reluctant participants, citing an emotional bond with the patient as the strongest motivation to engage in physician-assisted death. Requesters tended to be middle-aged rather than elderly, and men more than women. The act was most frequently done in the patient's own home, and was very infrequent in nursing homes.

Some of the data from this comprehensive survey are reassuring to those who advocate a cautious reappraisal of public policy in the United States. Though information about active euthanasia was commonly sought by patients, the procedure was carried out relatively infrequently. The elderly and nursing facility residents—persons frequently cited as potential targets of abuse—were relatively infrequent recipients of euthanasia. As in the United States, the vast majority of physician-assisted deaths was attributed to the double effects of narcotics and to nontreatment decisions (passive euthanasia) rather than active euthanasia. The study confirmed that unrelenting physical pain was infrequently the only problem leading to these requests. More commonly the request is motivated by a complex combination of personal and existential issues, mixed with physical suffering. It also confirmed that doctors remain reluctant about the process, but appear to participate because of compassion for their suffering patients.

Unfortunately, the translated review published in *The Lancet* provided little of the primary data, and little detail of the "exceptional" cases which would be helpful in ensuring a nonbiased review and presentation of the practice. The research was also completely dependent on the interviews and recorded practices of doctors, as opposed to information from patients, families, or independent observers. Although physicians were granted immunity from prosecution and their confidentiality was guaranteed, they may have been reluctant to report the details of exceptional cases. Despite these limitations and potential biases, the study suggests that the practice of euthanasia is considerably less frequent than had been speculated, and the vast majority of patients died within the accepted guidelines.

Before generalizing these findings to the United States, it is important to note that there is universal health care for all citizens in the Netherlands so that problems of unequal access do not confound the issue. Unlike the United States, there is also an extensive primary-care system, so that long-term, personal doctor-patient relationships are the rule rather than the exception. These differences make the risks of changing public policy in the Netherlands considerably less than in the United States.

INITIATIVES IN THE UNITED STATES

In 1988, a California initiative seeking to legalize euthanasia and physician-assisted suicide sponsored by Americans Against Human Suffering failed to gain enough signatures to become a ballot measure. Many believe that it failed more from inadequate organization than from a lack of public support. The initiative differed from the Dutch guidelines in two ways. First, to be eligible for physician-assisted death, the patient had to have a terminal prognosis, which was defined as less than six months. The Dutch guidelines require that the patient have an incurable illness associated with unrelenting suffering and no prospect for relief, but do not set a time limit on prognosis. Second, the California initiative would have allowed someone to select euthanasia by advance directive. Thus, a patient who had become incompetent would remain eligible provided he had executed a Living Will with explicit instructions, or had empowered a health-care agent to make that decision on his behalf. This allowed competent patients to ensure their death should they irreversibly lose mental capacity due to illness or accident in the future. This component of the initiative went considerably further than the Dutch guidelines in terms of loosening restrictions and eliminating safeguards. A similar initiative that combined assisted suicide and active voluntary euthanasia was defeated in California in November 1992. More restrictive initiatives including some that allow assisted suicide but not voluntary euthanasia are being considered in Florida, Oregon, and New Hampshire.

Perhaps the most well organized political campaign to change state law was Initiative 119 in Washington State. This proposal was backed by a broad coalition of mainstream physicians, clergy, lawyers, and patients, along with the Hemlock Society. Initiative 119 had three components. First, it defined "persistent vegetative state" as a terminal condition, and therefore allowed persons in such condition the same rights and privileges given to terminally ill patients. Second, it allowed feeding tubes to be removed from incompetent patients who had made their wishes known through an advance directive (Living Will or health care proxy) prior to losing competence. These two components of the legislation were not particularly controversial, and would simply catch the state of Washington up with much of the rest of the country in terms of protecting the rights of patients who lose competence to refuse treatment.

The third component of Initiative 119, however, would have broken very new ground in the United States by allowing patients to receive "aid in dying" (either active voluntary euthanasia or assisted suicide) from their physician, provided they could meet three conditions. First, aid in dying must be voluntarily requested by the patient. Second, the patient must be competent, and his/her decision making could not be distorted by depression or other mental disorder. Third, the patient must be terminally ill, defined as death expected within six months. The patient's prognosis had to be verified by two physicians, and a psychiatric evaluation was required if there were any question of incompetence.

This initiative passed through the legislature and became a ballot referendum in the fall of 1991. Though there was widespread public support for the general concept in the polls before the vote, the initiative was defeated by a 54 to 46 percent margin. Supporters attribute their defeat to several factors. While there were safeguards in the legislation, they were not comprehensive or explicit enough. In the last weeks prior to the vote there was a large infusion of money—primarily by national religious organizations—that was used to emphasize the inadequacy of the safeguards. That money fueled a misleading but effective media campaign which intensified fears about abuse (e.g., hospice nurses stating, "I would rather care for you than have to kill you"). In addition, though individual physicians in Washington were roughly equally divided on the issue, the State Medical Society vigorously opposed it. Many physicians feared an implicit obligation to assist their patients to die upon request, and were legitimately reluctant to enter this uncharted realm without extensive thought and guidance. Finally, in the last week before the vote, Dr. Kevorkian assisted two additional patients to commit suicide, enhancing fears about adequate safeguards and the potential for abuse. In spite of their narrow defeat, supporters of Initiative 119 believe that the majority of Washington State voters favor legislation in this area. They plan to reconstruct their initiative with tighter safeguards, and reintroduce it in the future.

Every public opinion poll over the last forty years about physicians taking a more active role in helping their terminally ill patients die has shown that the majority of the American public supports the idea. It is not known how widespread the current covert practice of physician-assisted dying is in the United States today. Since the practice remains largely secret and potentially legally and professionally punishable, accurate estimates of its prevalence are hard to obtain. Flawed surveys suggest that from 3 to 37 percent of anonymous physician respondents admit to having actively assisted at least one patient to die in their careers, yet how many times doctors actually have crossed the line into assisted suicide or active voluntary euthanasia is simply not known.

Independent surveys from the Hemlock Society, the University of Colorado, and the San Francisco Medical Society each suggest that a majority of physicians responding to such surveys favor some legalization of euthanasia under specified circumstances. However, some doctors who favored such legalization felt they would not want to participate in active euthanasia or assisted suicide themselves.

I have had the privilege of meeting several patients like Diane who have taken charge of their dying and death, and I have also witnessed and been told countless stories that vividly demonstrate the risks of current prohibitions. It has been argued that exceptional cases make bad law. Whereas I would agree that we need to anticipate and monitor the effects on a change in policy on everyday medical practice, it is not at all clear to me that these cases are exceptional or rare. I believe that we have heard about the tip of the iceberg in terms of the frequency, severity, and range of severe end-of-life suffering, and that only the most assertive and independent patients have been able to request and convince a doctor to actively assist them in dying. In my opinion, the benefits of cautiously changing public policy in response to the compelling need expressed by suffering patients and their families outweigh the risks—which, though formidable in theory, have yet to be convincingly demonstrated. For that reason, I believe that we should cautiously explore allowing physician-assisted suicide under carefully controlled conditions. My view of the risks and benefits of this change in policy, as well as clinically relevant safeguards, is presented in the next chapter.

Chapter 8

PHYSICIAN-ASSISTED SUICIDE

Potential Clinical Criteria

*T*he clinical criteria presented in this chapter were developed in collaboration with Dr. Christine Cassel, Professor of Medicine and Public Policy from the University of Chicago, and Dr. Diane Meier, Associate Professor of Medicine and Geriatrics at The Mount Sinai Medical School in New York. As background, we used readings from the medical, philosophical, ethical, legal, and public policy literatures, along with our collective clinical and personal experience. The criteria were originally presented in an article in the New England Journal of Medicine entitled "Care of the Hopelessly Ill: Potential Clinical Criteria for Physician Assisted Suicide" (NEJM 1992; 327:1380–84), which is partially reproduced in the first half of this chapter.* The criteria represent our best efforts to increase the options available to incurably ill patients, while defining clear safeguards to prevent misuse. By formally presenting these potential criteria we wanted to achieve three goals: (1) To provide some guidance for physicians and patients who are considering such options. (2) To promote

*The references have been taken out for easier reading, but all works that went into the article can be found within the Bibliography.

continued, open discussion about potential clinical criteria and safeguards for physician-assisted suicide. (3) To help guide policy makers and legislators who are considering formal changes in public policy or the law.

CARE OF THE HOPELESSLY ILL:
POTENTIAL CLINICAL CRITERIA FOR
PHYSICIAN-ASSISTED SUICIDE

One of medicine's highest missions is to allow hopelessly ill persons to die with as much comfort, control, and dignity as possible. The philosophy and techniques of comfort care provide a humane alternative to more traditional, curative medical approaches that can help patients to achieve this end. Yet there remain troubling instances where incurably ill patients suffer intolerably prior to death in spite of comprehensive efforts to provide comfort care. Some of these patients reach a point where they would rather die than continue living under the conditions imposed by their illness, and a few request assistance from their physicians.

The patients who ask us to face their tragic dilemma do not fall into simple diagnostic categories. Until recently, their problem has been relatively unacknowledged and unexplored by the medical profession, so there is little objectively known about its spectrum and prevalence, or about the range of physician responses. Yet each unique request can be compelling:

• A former athlete, weighing 80 pounds after an eight-year struggle with acquired immunodeficiency syndrome (AIDS), who is losing his sight and his memory, and is terrified of AIDS dementia.

- A mother of seven children, continually exhausted and bed-bound at home with a gaping, foul-smelling, open wound in her abdomen, who can no longer eat, and who no longer finds any meaning in her fight against ovarian cancer.
- A fiercely independent retired factory worker, quadriplegic from amyotrophic lateral sclerosis, who no longer wants to linger in a helpless, dependent state waiting and hoping for death.
- A writer with extensive bony metastases from lung cancer, having not responded to chemotherapy or radiation, who cannot accept the daily choice he must make between sedation or severe pain.
- A physician colleague, dying of respiratory failure from progressive pulmonary fibrosis, who doesn't want to go onto a ventilator, but is also terrified of suffocation.

Like the case of "Diane," which has been told in more depth, there are personal stories of courage and grief behind each of these images that force us to take their requests for a physician's assistance very seriously. It is for competent, incurably ill patients such as these who have no escape other than death that this discussion is being opened.

The purpose of this paper is to present potential clinical criteria that, if met, would allow physicians to openly and safely respond to requests from their competent, incurably ill patients for assisted suicide. We support legalization of physician-assisted suicide, but not active euthanasia, as the correct balance of humane response to the requests of patients like those outlined above, and protection of other vulnerable populations. We strongly advocate the principles and practices of intensive, unrestrained comfort care for all incurably ill persons. When properly applied, comfort care should result in meaningful, tolerable, and relatively symptom-controlled deaths for most patients. Physician-assisted suicide should never be contemplated as a substitute for comprehensive comfort care, or for joining with patients to find unique solutions for the physical, personal, and social challenges posed by the difficult process of dying. Yet it is neither idiosyncratic, selfish, or emblematic of a psychiatric disorder for a person with an incurable illness to want to have some control over how he leaves this world. A noble, dignified death is exalted in great literature, poetry, art, and music, and its meaning is deeply personal and unique. When an incurably ill patient asks for help achieving a dignified death, we believe that physicians have an obligation to fully explore the request, and, under specified circumstances, to carefully consider making an exception to the prohibition against assisting suicide.

Physician-Assisted Suicide

Physician-assisted suicide is defined as the act of making a means of suicide (such as a prescription for barbiturates) available to a patient who is otherwise physically capable of suicide, and who subsequently acts on his or her own. It is distinguished from voluntary euthanasia where the physician not only makes the means available, but is the actual agent of death upon the patient's request. Whereas active euthanasia is uniformly illegal in the United States, only thirty-six states have laws explicitly prohibiting assisted suicide. In every situation where a physician has compassionately assisted a terminally ill person to commit suicide, criminal charges have been dismissed or a verdict of not guilty found. Though the reality of successful prosecution may be remote, the risk of an expensive, publicized professional and legal inquiry will be prohibitive for most physicians, and will certainly keep the practice covert and isolating for those who participate.

It is not known how widespread the secret practice of physician-assisted suicide is currently in the United States, nor how frequently patients' requests to physicians are turned down. Approximately 6,000 deaths per day are in some way planned or indirectly assisted in the United States, probably confined to the "double effect" of pain-relieving medications, and to discontinuing or not starting potentially life-prolonging treatments. Survey data that are flawed by low response rates and poor design suggest that from 3 to 37 percent of anonymously responding physicians admitted secretly taking active steps to hasten a patient's death. Every public opinion survey taken over the past forty years asking questions about physician-assisted dying for the terminally ill has shown that a majority of Americans support the idea. A referendum with loosely defined safeguards that would have legalized both voluntary euthanasia and assisted suicide was narrowly defeated in Washington State in 1991, and more conservatively drawn initiatives are currently on the ballot in California, before the legislature in New Hampshire, and under consideration in Florida and Oregon.

A Policy Proposal

While both physician-assisted suicide and voluntary euthanasia have as their common intent the active facilitation of a wished-for death, there are several important distinctions between them. In assisted suicide, the final act is solely the patient's, thus greatly reducing the risk of subtle coercion from doctors, family members, institutions, or other social forces. The balance of power between doctor and patient is more nearly equal in physician-assisted suicide. The physician is counselor and witness, and makes the means available, but ultimately the patient must act or not act on his own. With voluntary euthanasia, the physician must provide both the means and the actual conduct of the final act, greatly amplifying the physician's power over the patient, and increasing the risk of error, coercion, or abuse.

In view of these distinctions, we have concluded that legalization of physician-assisted suicide, but not voluntary euthanasia, is the policy option best able to both respond to and protect this vulnerable population. From this perspective, physician-assisted suicide would be part of a continuum of comfort care options, beginning with foregoing life-sustaining therapy, coupled with aggressive symptom-relieving measures, and permitting physician-assisted suicide only if all other alternatives have failed and all criteria are met. Active voluntary euthanasia would be excluded from this continuum because of the risk of abuse. We recognize that this exclusion occurs at a cost to those competent, incurably ill patients who are unable to swallow or to move, and who therefore could not be helped to die by assisted suicide. Such persons who otherwise meet agreed-upon criteria must not be abandoned to their suffering: a combination of decisions to forego life-sustaining treatments (including food and fluids) with aggressive comfort measures (such as analgesics and sedatives) could be offered, along with a commitment to search for creative alternatives. We acknowledge that this is a less than ideal solution, but also recognize that access to medical care in the United States currently is too inequitable and many doctor-patient relationships too impersonal to tolerate the risks of condoning active voluntary euthanasia. We must study and monitor any change in public policy in this domain to evaluate both its benefits and burdens.

We propose the following clinical guidelines to stimulate serious discussion about permitting physician-assisted suicide. Though we favor a reconsideration of the legal and professional prohibitions for patients who clearly meet carefully defined criteria, we do not wish to promote an easy or impersonal process. If we are to consider allowing incurably ill patients more control over their deaths, it must be as an expression of our compassion and concern about the ultimate fate of those who have exhausted all other alternatives. Such patients should not be held hostage to our reluctance or inability to forge policies in this difficult terrain.

Potential Clinical Criteria for Physician-Assisted Suicide

Because assisted suicide is extraordinary and irreversible treatment, the patient's primary physician must ensure the conditions set forth below are clearly satisfied before proceeding:

1. *The patient must, of his own free will and at his own initiative, clearly and repeatedly request to die rather than continue suffering.* The physician should have a thorough understanding of what continued life would mean to the patient and on what basis the patient deems death preferable. A physician's too-ready acceptance of a patient's request could be perceived as encouragement to commit suicide, yet we also don't want to be so prohibitive or reticent that the patient is forced to "beg" for assistance. Understanding the patient's desire to die and ensuring that the request is enduring are critical in evaluating the patient's rationality, and in assuring that all alternative means of relieving suffering have been adequately explored. Any sign of patient ambivalence or uncertainty should abort the process, as a clear, convincing, and continuous desire for an end of suffering through death is a strict requirement to proceed. Requests for assisted suicide by advance directive or by a health care surrogate should not be honored.

2. *The patient's judgment must not be distorted.* The patient must be capable of understanding the decision and its implications and consequences. The presence of depression is relevant if it is distorting rational decision making and is reversible in a way that would substantially alter the situation. Expert psychiatric evaluation should be sought when the primary physician is inex-

perienced in the diagnosis and treatment of depression, or when there is any uncertainty about the rationality of the request or the presence of a reversible mental disorder that would substantially change the patient's perception of his condition once treated.

3. The patient must have a condition that is incurable, and associated with severe, unrelenting, intolerable suffering. The patient must understand his condition, prognosis, and the comfort care alternatives available. Though we anticipate that most patients making this request will be imminently terminal, we acknowledge the inexactness of such prognostications, and do not want to arbitrarily exclude persons with incurable, but not imminently terminal, progressive illnesses such as ALS or multiple sclerosis. When there is considerable uncertainty about the patient's medical condition or prognosis, second opinions should be sought and the uncertainty clarified as much as possible before a final response to the patient's request is made.

4. The physician must ensure that the patient's suffering and the request are not the result of inadequate comfort care. All reasonable comfort-oriented measures must have been at least considered, and preferably tried, before providing the means for a physician-assisted suicide. Physician-assisted suicide must never be used to circumvent the struggle to provide comprehensive comfort care, or find acceptable alternatives. The physician's willingness to provide assisted suicide in the future is legitimate and important to discuss if raised by the patient, since many will probably find the potential of an escape more important than the reality.

5. Physician-assisted suicide should only be carried out in the context of a meaningful doctor-patient relationship. This relationship should not be based solely on the patient's request for assisted suicide. Ideally, the physician should have witnessed the patient's prior illness and suffering. Though a preexisting relationship may not always be possible, the aiding physician must get to know the patient personally, so that the reasons for the request are fully understood. The physician must understand why, from the patient's perspective, death is the best of a limited number of very unfortunate options. The primary physician must personally confirm each of the criteria. The patient should have no doubt about the physician's commitment to find alternative solutions with him if at any moment he changes his mind. Rather than creating a new death subspeciality, assisted suicide should be provided by the same physician who is struggling with the patient to find comfort care alternatives, and will stand by the patient and provide care for him until his death no matter what path is taken.

No physician should be forced to assist a patient in suicide if it violates her fundamental values, though the patient's personal physician should think deeply before turning down the patient's request. Should transfer of care be necessary, the patient's personal physician should help the patient find another more receptive primary physician.

6. *Consultation with another experienced physician is required* to ensure the voluntariness and rationality of the patient's request, the accuracy of the diagnosis and prognosis, and the full exploration of comfort-oriented alternatives. The consulting physician should review the supporting materials, and personally interview and examine the patient.

7. *Clear documentation to support each condition above is required.* A system must be developed for reporting, reviewing, studying, and clearly distinguishing such deaths from other forms of suicide. The patient, the primary physician, and the consultant must each sign a consent form. A physician-assisted suicide must neither invalidate insurance policies, nor lead to a medical examiner investigation or an unwanted autopsy. The primary physician, the medical consultant, and the involved family must have assurance

that, if the agreed upon conditions are satisfied in good faith, they will be free from criminal prosecution for their role in assisting the patient to die.

Informing family members is strongly recommended, but final control over whom to involve and inform is left to the discretion and control of the patient. Similarly, spiritual counseling should be offered, depending on the patient's background and beliefs. Ideally, close family members are integrally involved in the decision-making process, and should understand and support the patient's decision. If there is an unresolvable dispute about how to proceed between the family and patient, such matters may need involvement of an ethics committee, or even the courts. However, it is hoped that most of these painful decisions can be worked through directly between the patient, family, and health-care providers. Under no circumstances should the wishes and requests of the family override those of a competent patient.

Method: The main method used in physician-assisted suicide is the prescription of a lethal amount of medication which the patient then ingests on his own. Since assisted suicide has been a covert, largely unstudied process, little is known about the most humane and effective methods. If there is a change in policy, there must be an open sharing of information about methods within the profession, and a careful analysis of effectiveness. The methods selected should be 100 percent effective, and should not contribute to further patient suffering. We must also provide support systems and careful monitoring for the patients, physicians, and families who participate, since the emotional and social effects are largely unknown, but undoubtedly far reaching.

Physician-assisted suicide is one of the most profound and meaningful acts that a patient can ask of his physician. If both the patient and the physician agree that there are no acceptable alternatives and that all the required conditions are met, the lethal medication should ideally be taken in the presence of the patient's physician. Unless the patient specifically requests it, he should not be left alone at the time of death. In addition to the personal physician, other health-care providers and family members whom the patient wishes should be encouraged to be present. The principle of not abandoning the patient is of utmost importance at this critical moment. The time before a controlled death can provide an opportunity for a rich and meaningful goodbye between family members, health-care providers, and the patient. In this context, we must be sure that any policies and laws enacted to allow assisted suicide do not require that the patient be alone at the moment of death in order for the assisters to be safe from prosecution.

Balancing Risks and Benefits

There is an intensifying debate within and outside of the medical profession about the physician's appropriate role in assisting dying. While most will agree that there are exceptional circumstances where death would be preferable to intolerable suffering, the case against physician-assisted suicide (and voluntary euthanasia) is based mainly on its implications for public policy and its potential impact on the moral integrity of the medical profession. The "slippery slope" argument suggests permissive policies would inevitably lead to subtle coercion of the powerless to choose death rather than become a burden on society or their family. Access to health care in the United States is extraordinarily variable, often impersonal, and subject to intense cost-containment pressures. It may be dangerous to license physicians to take life in this unstable environment. It is also suggested that skillfully applied comfort care could provide a tolerable and dignified death for most persons, and that the incentive for the physician to become more proficient at comfort care would be less if the option of a quick, controlled death were too readily available. Finally, some believe that physician-assisted death, no matter how noble and pure its intentions, could destroy the identity of the medical profession and its central ethos of protecting the sanctity of life. The question before policy makers, physicians, and voters is whether criteria such as those we have outlined in this paper adequately safeguard patients against these risks.

The risks and burdens of continuing with current prohibitions have been less clearly articulated in the literature. The most pressing problem is the potential abandonment of those competent, incurably ill patients who yearn for death rather than continuing a life without meaning or hope, in spite of comprehensively applied comfort care. These patients have sometimes used medical treatments to extend their lives to the point that they are both physically and emotionally falling apart, but not imminently dying. Those who have witnessed difficult deaths of patients on hospice programs are not reassured by the glib assertion that we always know how to make death tolerable, and they fear that physicians will abandon them if their course becomes difficult or overwhelming in the face of comfort care. In fact, there is no empirical evidence that all physical suffering associated with incurable illness can be effectively relieved. In addition, for many the most frightening aspect of death is not physical pain, but the prospect of losing control and independence, and dying in an undignified, unesthetic, absurd, and existentially unacceptable condition.

Those physicians who respond to the requests for assisted suicide by these patients do so at substantial professional and legal peril, often acting in secret out of compassion without the benefit of consultation or support from colleagues. This covert practice discourages open and honest communication between physicians, their colleagues, and their dying patients. Decisions are often dependent more on the physician's values and willingness to take risk than the compelling nature of the patient's request. There may be more risk for abuse and idiosyncratic decision-making with such secret practices than with a more open, carefully defined practice. Finally, those terminally ill patients who do choose to take their life often die alone so as not to legally jeopardize their families or caregivers.

Conclusion

Given current professional and legal prohibitions, physicians find themselves in a difficult position when faced with requests for assisted suicide by suffering patients who have exhausted comfort care measures. To adhere to the letter of the law, they must turn down their patients' requests even if they find them reasonable and personally acceptable. To accede to their patients' requests, they must risk violating legal and professional standards, and therefore act in isolation and secret collaboration with their patients. It is our opinion that there is more risk for vulnerable patients and for the integrity of the profession in such hidden practices, however well intended, than there would be in a more open process restricted to competent patients who met carefully defined criteria. The professions of medicine and law must collaborate if we are to create public policy that fully acknowledges irreversible end-of-life suffering, and offers dying patients a broader range of options for exploration with their physicians.

DIANE'S DEATH UNDER THIS POLICY

How would Diane's illness or death have been altered if this policy were in place? We can first determine if she would have met all seven conditions, and then speculate about how she, her family, and I as her physician would have been helped by a more open process. If a change in public policy is seriously contemplated, it is vital to explore its effects on actual patients such as Diane who would clearly seem to benefit from this option. Only by exploring a policy's effect on real people can we realistically determine whether the benefits of a change outweigh the burdens.

All seven criteria for physician-assisted suicide must be clearly satisfied before it would be sanctioned under the proposed guidelines. I will now consider the implications of each criterion on Diane's case.

1. *The patient must, of her own free will and at her own initiative, clearly and repeatedly request to die rather than continue suffering.* Diane was a person of strong will and clear opinions who was not about to be controlled or overly influenced by others. The initial idea was hers alone, and I as her physician was reluctant and skeptical. Yet her request to die was consistent with her long-standing values and beliefs, and her motivation to avoid lingering near death at the end in a state that she would have found meaningless was clearly stated and unambiguous. She was clear and consistent about the circumstances under which she would want to end her life, and when she came to that point, her commitment was unwavering. As we reviewed what comfort care could offer at the end, she remained clear that death was now far preferable to lingering for hours, days, or weeks in relative "comfort."

2. *The patient's judgment must not be distorted.* I said in my original article that Diane was an "incredibly clear, brutally honest" thinker. There was no doubt in the minds of any of the professional or lay people who were fortunate enough to spend time with Diane over the last three months that her judgment was intact. Diane faced death directly and openly, and could explore

the implications of each of her decisions with a clarity and sophis-
tication that impressed everyone she met. This is not to say that
she was not sad or discouraged at times in her illness, for she was
not at all eager to leave this life. But her fear of lingering and
dependence at the end outweighed her fear of death. She believed
in her own way in an afterlife, and the imagery of Lake Geneva at
sunset gave her great solace. Diane's resolve remained consistent
for the three months that she lived after her diagnosis, and she
fulfilled her part of our agreement to meet with me prior to taking
her life to ensure that all alternatives had been explored. In that
sad visit, as Diane faced death and I faced my inability to change
the inevitable, it was tragically clear that there were no good alternatives. Superficial solutions seemed trivial, and the mandate not
to abandon my patient became paramount. What this meant to
me was to give her as much choice and control as possible, given
the severe limits of the options available.

   *3. The patient must have a condition that is incurable, and as-
sociated with severe, unrelenting, intolerable suffering.* There could
conceivably be some debate about whether Diane would meet
this criterion. Acute leukemia is potentially curable, but only if
one is willing to undertake very severe medical treatment with
relatively poor odds. Since patients have the unequivocal right to
refuse medical treatment, even if that treatment might be life-
saving, we cannot then punish those who do so by not offering
them treatments intended to humanize their dying. At the time of
her diagnosis, Diane had seen several independent oncologists to
ensure that she knew what she was giving up. There was no
question in each consultant's mind that she had a full understanding of the options and their implications. Three months later,
when Diane took her life, her acute leukemia was incurable and
her suffering had become intolerable to her. Not only was acute
medical treatment unacceptable, but at the end, traditional comfort care measures offered little of value to Diane. In her eyes,

since death was inevitable, why subject herself to the humiliation of total physical and emotional dependence on others for her last moments?

4. *The physician must ensure that the patient's suffering and the request are not the result of inadequate comfort care.* Diane spent three months in a hospice program from the time she was diagnosed to her death. During much of that time she had enough medication to potentially take her life, but she had made a personal commitment not to use it for that purpose without meeting with me first to ensure that all other comfort-oriented options had been exhausted. She had several life-prolonging and comfort-enhancing medical interventions during that period. Several of her severe infections responded surprisingly well to oral antibiotics. When she became severely fatigued from anemia, she was briefly admitted to the inpatient hospice unit for transfusions which gave her a short boost in energy. Her bone pain from the leukemia was well controlled by an oral narcotic medication. She was wonderfully supported by her husband, who began doing much of his work from home, and her son, who took a semester off from school in order to be close to his mother. She was regularly seen by her hospice nurse and by her closest friends.

Diane and her family grew closer during her time on the hospice program. In those three months she experienced the best that comfort care has to offer—good control of her physical symptoms, excellent emotional and social support, and intimate, healing contact with family and friends. Toward the end of the three months, however, the quality of her life began to dissipate. High fevers persisted despite antibiotics, weakness progressed in the face of repeated transfusions, the increased narcotic pain medications needed to control her pain made her sleepy, and the leukemia progressively invaded her skin, which became sore, red, and swollen. She became so weak that walking even a few steps was an ordeal.

In her eyes, continuing life under such circumstances lacked any meaning. She had made peace with herself, and resolved all that was resolvable with her family and close friends. Her future now held only the terrifying prospect of increasing dependence, incapacity, and loss of integrity prior to death. Death was far preferable to Diane than enduring the further dissolution of all that had meaning to her, and there was nothing more that comfort care could do to ease what was becoming an excruciating final decline. Though Diane clearly benefited from comfort care for three months, toward the end it was not enough to ensure a dignified death. I believe that if she had not had the assurance of a controlled death when her suffering became intolerable, much of the quality of the three months that she did have would have been contaminated by fear and by searching for a potential way out. She might even have taken an earlier escape through suicide, since she would have had to fear becoming too weak to act on her own if she waited too long.

5. Physician-assisted suicide should only be carried out in the context of a meaningful doctor-patient relationship. Diane and I had an eight-year relationship that had weathered other storms. Though a preexisting relationship is not a requirement, in-depth knowledge of the patient's request and the motivation behind it is extremely important. Our relationship was in no way contingent on her decision about suicide. We were committed to working together until her death, no matter which course she chose and which direction her illness took us. Diane's family was fully informed and involved in the decision making. After extensive discussions, they agreed that the decisions about treatment and potential suicide were hers to make. Although we all wished that Diane was not critically ill and dying, given her fierce independence, her request not to linger at the end was in no way surprising.

Diane's request was also not inconsistent with my own personal values. I have seen considerable end-of-life suffering, both in my work as a hospice medical director and as a primary-care physician, which could have been lessened by a wider range of physician options to ease the passage into death. If, as a patient, I personally faced increasing helplessness and indignity that could only end with my death, I would seriously consider putting an end to my life. Though I don't know what I would do, I would clearly want (and have because I am a physician) the option of a controlled and dignified death. In my deliberations, I learned that assisted suicide was illegal, but covertly tolerated by the law (that no case had been successfully prosecuted) and by the medical profession, provided it is kept secret and indirect. After several discussions with Diane and her family, I elected to remain true to my personal values and to take a professional risk. I want to emphasize that I did this out of my own free will, under no pressure from Diane. However, had I been unwilling to help her, she would have had to carefully consider other methods to act on her own.

6. *Consultation with another experienced physician is required.* Shortly after her initial diagnosis, Diane saw two separate oncologists from two different institutions to ensure that she understood her disease and the implications of her refusal of treatment. She also discussed her situation briefly with a psychologist whom she had worked with extensively in the past. In addition, the medical director of the home hospice program (the job I held in the past) was informally consulted, as she is on all hospice cases to ensure that every measure that might enhance patient comfort is being considered. There was no doubt that Diane fully understood her situation, and no questions were raised by any health-care providers about her judgment or rationality. She clearly received the best that comfort care had to offer.

Because of the potential illegality of assisted suicide, the consultations that I obtained pertaining to Diane's request for a controlled death were more informal and confidential, but extremely helpful nonetheless. As I contemplated crossing a frightening boundary that I had never crossed before, it was important for me to ensure that my own thinking was rational, and that I had fully considered all other options and alternatives. Ideally, such consultants would confirm adherence to the prestated criteria by reviewing data recorded by the primary physician, and also by meeting directly with the patient and even the family to independently confirm the key elements. Such a direct consultation would be much more valuable than the indirect consultations that I received, though the support and consultation that I received were far preferable to a doctor and a patient acting in complete secrecy and isolation.

7. Clear documentation to support each condition above is required. Just as it is difficult to get an in-depth second opinion about a practice that is potentially illegal and on the ethical edge of appropriate physician behavior, clearly documenting the data supporting the decisions is also dangerous. Thus, Diane's medical record contains a detailed account of the reasoning behind her refusal of medical treatment for acute leukemia (an accepted though controversial decision, given current medical standards), but no mention of her considerations about suicide, or my thinking about my potential role in indirectly assisting her. Requiring careful, systematic documentation to show that the criteria were met prior to allowing physician-assisted suicide would clearly bring the decision making more out in the open, and allow the supporting data to be reviewed by outside observers. Diane would have been more than willing to sign a consent form. She clearly could have met all the criteria, and therefore could have been assisted without all the secrecy. Helping Diane to die with dignity in the face of her relentless illness was challenging and emotionally wrenching enough without these added impediments.

In addition to more open documentation in the patient's medical record and a formal consent form, a mechanism for recording such deaths on a death certificate, and for distinguishing them from suicides stemming from depression and other mental ill-nesses, would also be needed. Patients and their families would need reassurance that life insurance policies would not be in-validated by such acts, and that the stigma associated with other suicide deaths would be minimized. I was severely criticized for recording "acute leukemia" as the cause of death on Diane's death certificate, yet suicide would not have even been a remote question to her had she not been dying of leukemia. Any mention of suicide to the medical examiner or the funeral director would have led to an immediate call to an ambulance crew to try cardi-opulmonary resuscitation, in spite of the fact Diane had already been dead for several hours. This unwarranted and unwanted assault would then have been followed by an interrogation of the family by the medical examiner to determine their possible role in the death, and an unwanted autopsy to establish with certainty if medication contributed to her death. Such an invasion of Diane's body and of her family's potential role in her death would have violated fundamental principles of humane care of the dying, as well as all that we were working together to achieve in terms of allowing Diane a dignified, partially controlled death. My obliga-tion to Diane and her family seemed to outweigh my obligation to share the full complexity of her death with the medical examiner. Designation of the immediate cause of death is notoriously inaccu-rate under the best of circumstances. Whether or not the medical examiner would have differentiated between Diane's death and a suicide stemming from mental illness, in my opinion her death resulted much more from her leukemia. The overdose of medica-tion that she took probably shortened her life by at most a few days to a week.

Ironically, under media pressure to determine exactly who Diane was in the wake of my article describing her illness and death, her full name was identified by an anonymous tip. Her body, which she had generously given to science for medical edu-cation and research, was eventually located by the district attor-ney. Without the family's permission, it was confiscated, and an unwanted autopsy was performed that "proved" that the immediate cause of her death was an overdose of medication. I was told that, had Diane been buried when she died, she would have been exhumed without the family's permission as part of the medical examiner's inquiry. Unfortunately, Diane's family went through a very public interrogation because of the article—the exact processes that I had tried to protect them from. Though Diane's family and I jointly reached the original decision that Diane would have wanted her story to be told, none of us had anticipated the seemingly absurd lengths that the legal inquiry would take.

The notion that we can allow such violations of dying patients and their families who dare to take some small measure of control over death still mystifies and infuriates me. I feel angry and sad that Diane and her family had to suffer through this added humiliation after already losing so much. I just hope that we all can learn from their experience.

The most tragic aspect of the story for Diane herself is that she died alone. Diane was correct in her assumption that the grand jury would find my role too ambiguous to prosecute if she were alone at her death. Yet, as physicians, we make a commitment to our dying patients not to abandon them no matter how difficult or overwhelming their situation may become. Patients would not feel they would have to put their doctor and family at risk to be with them at the time of death if assisted suicide were more open and legalized. Family members, friends, and the doctor could all say goodbye to the patient, and then freely remain together during the patient's waning moments. Enhancing patient choice and control while minimizing abandonment and isolation are probably the most compelling reasons for considering a change in public policy. The costs of the current prohibitions—uncontrolled suffering, increased dependence on the physician's values rather than the patient's, idiosyncratic, secretive behavior on the part of the physician, and abandonment of the patient—are so high that serious consideration of a change in policy is imperative.

Chapter 9

BACKGROUND FOR ADVANCE DIRECTIVES

What Can Happen If I Lose Mental Capacity in the Future?

As long as patients have full mental capacity, they retain the right to accept or refuse any medical treatment. But what happens if a patient loses the mental capacity to make these decisions? If the loss is temporary, and the patient has not clearly specified otherwise, the medical obligation is to use all potentially effective measures to prolong life until the patient has recovered enough to make his or her wishes known. If patients become *permanently* mentally impaired without letting their wishes be known, their rights to refuse or to withdraw life-prolonging medical treatment are in serious jeopardy.

The task of those who are empowered to make decisions on behalf of an incompetent patient is to try to use *the patient's own values and statements* to try to make decisions as the patient would have made them. In ethical terminology, this is called "substituted judgment." Substituted judgment is not available to those who have never had the capacity to let their wishes be known, such as infants or those with profound mental retardation. Though some patients who lose their ability to make decisions have made clear statements in the past that apply to the circumstances in which they find themselves, more often there is at least some uncertainty about exactly what their wishes might be. In the face of this uncertainty, incompetent patients are often assumed to want all life-prolonging treatments that they have not specifically refused in the past.

Let me illustrate some of the effects of this presumption through several real cases. I hope these stories will encourage you to complete an advance directive if you have not already done so. Advance directives are formal documents that are completed when one has full mental capacity, and are intended to guide medical treatment in case one loses the ability to speak for oneself in the future. Two advance directive options, the Living Will and the Health Care Proxy, will be described in detail in the next chapter, and sample forms are included in the Appendix. If you think the stories that I am about to tell are rare, you are mistaken. I advise you to discuss this issue with your doctor and your family, and to take a careful look around you the next time that you visit an intensive-care unit, an acute-care hospital, or a nursing facility.

MARK

Mark was the young man with the severe heart disease described in Chapter 2 who had a cardiac arrest at home. Tragically, his body survived but his brain did not. Though there was no question from his neurologic examination and from his electroencephalogram that Mark was severely and permanently brain-damaged, he did not meet the medical criteria for brain death (his brain had a small amount of very disorganized electrical activity). Had Mark been a typical nine-teen-year-old who had not thought about these issues and let his wishes be known in advance, how would we have proceeded? We would first have met with his family to try to help them understand and begin to accept the terrible situation. Eventually, we would explore with them whether Mark had made his wishes known in any way about this kind of circumstance. Since most nineteen-year-olds think of death only as something that happens to someone else, more often than not we would get no definite direction from this inquiry.

Without a past statement by the patient that applies to the current situation, we would then try to infer what we think he would have wanted. Here the ground is less certain. Sometimes indirect evidence about the patient's values or their approach to other problems can help generate an educated guess, but there is often considerable uncertainty as to whether such predictions accurately reflect the patient's wishes. What we as individual physicians or family members would want in the other person's situation is even less reliable. "Reasonable persons" differ substantially about their wishes at the end of life. In the absence of clear evidence that incompetent patients would not have wanted life-prolonging treatment, they are much more likely than not to get all available life-prolonging medical treatments, no matter what their quality of life or prognosis for recovery.

Fortunately, Mark had made his wishes known in no uncertain terms. Not only had he refused a recommended, potentially life-prolonging intervention in the past (an implanted permanent defibrillator), but he had clearly articulated his preference for death over a life without full consciousness or the potential for physical independence. Five days after his cardiac arrest, as Mark lay motionless in the intensive-care unit, kept alive by a breathing machine and a multitude of other life-supporting interventions, his mother, father, and I faced the overwhelming decision about whether to discontinue life-prolonging treatment. We each had to try to separate our own grief and our wishes that things would have turned out differently, and focus on the task at hand: What would Mark want us to do if he were still in control of the decision?

Though Mark had not executed a formal advance directive, he had let his wishes be known to each of us after his earlier cardiac arrest. *His wishes were reflected in a paper he had written in school about the "right to die." He wrote: "If a person is in a comatose state and doesn't have any way to respond, put yourself in their shoes or bed and try to imagine what it would be like. I'm sure everyone would choose death over total numbness, physically and mentally. . . . Incredible new medical technology has made it possible to keep people alive even if the brain is irretrievably damaged or lung and heart are incapable of functioning without mechanical help. It's an unnatural effort to keep someone alive . . . against their will."*

Given our shared knowledge about Mark's unambiguous wishes, our mandate to discontinue treatment was clear. We no longer had to continue aggressive medical treatment until there were signs of complete brain death, but rather could discontinue life-prolonging treatments and treat Mark with principles of comfort care. Not only were we on solid ground from a medicolegal perspective, but Mark's family and I could make this decision without the added burden of uncertainty and guilt as to whether we were carrying out Mark's will. By clearly articulating his wishes, Mark was able to ensure that he was not kept alive in a permanent "coma," and he also freed his family from adding guilt to their profound grief about letting go of their son. Even worse for Mark, had his parents not been strong enough to let go, he might have been kept alive for days, weeks, or even months against wishes that he could no longer express. Instead, those who loved him said their final goodbyes, and all treatments not purely related to his comfort were stopped. Mark peacefully died within a matter of minutes, with his parents by his side.

It was heartbreaking and unfair to lose Mark at such a young age, yet he was still able to assert his will at the end and thereby die with dignity in the face of this tragedy. Had he not faced death so squarely while fully alive, and let his wishes be clearly known, his end could have been humiliating rather than healing both for him and his family. Instead, Mark was allowed to live and die on his own terms.

NANCY CRUZAN

Much has been written and discussed about the heroic struggle that Nancy Cruzan's family waged against the state of Missouri and ultimately the United State's Supreme Court to allow their daughter to discontinue a life-sustaining feeding tube. Those of you who have not completed an advance directive should read this story carefully. If you continue to avoid the issue, such a fate could befall you and your family. I have no personal knowledge of the Cruzans, and am reconstructing the story from extensive published reports and analysis of the case.

In 1983, Nancy Cruzan, then in her mid-twenties, was severely injured in an auto accident. With the help of extensive, invasive medical measures, including the initial use of cardiopulmonary resuscitation, Ms. Cruzan survived. Unfortunately, she emerged from the process with severe brain damage, incapable of higher brain functions and unaware of her surroundings. Since she could not eat, a permanent feeding tube was surgically placed into her stomach to mechanically provide hydration and nutrition. (I will use the terms "feeding tube" and "artificial hydration and nutrition" interchangeably in the subsequent discussion to describe this life-sustaining treatment.) Because the rest of her body survived the accident relatively intact, she could be sustained indefinitely in this state (a "persistent vegetative state") as long as the tube feedings were continued. Her parents hoped she would get better, and waited for four years before reluctantly accepting that she would not recover. Then, out of love for their daughter and respect for what they felt would be her wishes, her parents formally petitioned the courts to allow removal of the feeding tube. They based the petition partially on their daughter's statements that she would not want to go on living if she could not be "at least halfway normal."

An initial lower court judge supported the parents' request, but the case was appealed to the Missouri Supreme Court where the decision was overturned. The court reasoned that the state had a legitimate interest in protecting the sanctity of life, and that "clear and convincing evidence" about the patient's own wish to forgo artificial hydration and nutrition was required in order to withhold the feedings or remove the feeding tube. It was their determination that Ms. Cruzan's general statements in the past such as not wishing to be "kept alive as a vegetable" were not specific enough to cover artificial hydration and nutrition. There was no question in the court's mind that the family had their daughter's best interest in mind, nor that they were trying to use their knowledge of their daughter's statements and values to guide the decision. In effect, the court was saying that the state's interest in protecting the sanctity of life could overrule a caring family's attempts to make decisions on behalf of their incompetent family member using "substituted judgment" in the area of artificial hydration and nutrition. Unless the patient had made her wishes known about the specific treatment *in a "clear and convincing" way, even a loving family member could not refuse it on her behalf.*

The case was eventually presented to the United States Supreme Court. This was the first time that the Supreme Court formally addressed the rights of competent or incompetent patients to refuse life-sustaining treatment. As background for the case, there was a substantial body of case law from lower courts supporting the rights of competent patients to refuse life-sustaining treatment. A growing number of legal decisions had begun to allow surrogate decision makers to refuse treatment on behalf of incompetent patients, including artificial hydration and nutrition, even if such decisions would indirectly result in the death of the patient.

The Supreme Court unfortunately rejected the appeal by Nancy Cruzan's parents. Though they supported the right of a competent patient to refuse any treatment, the Court ruled that the Constitution did not prohibit a state's placing restrictions on the rights of surrogates to make decisions on behalf of incompetent patients. They felt that there was nothing unconstitutional about requiring "clear and convincing" evidence of patients' wishes in order to allow their families or loved ones to withhold or withdraw artificial nutrition and hydration on their behalf. The Supreme Court supported the state's right to use this standard to require continued treatment with artificial hydration and nutrition for Nancy Cruzan, overruling her wishes as expressed through the substituted judgments of her parents. By not having specifically articulated her wishes about artificial hydration and nutrition while she was still healthy, Nancy Cruzan was not allowed to refuse that treatment through a surrogate once she became mentally incompetent. Thus, while family members are allowed to make decisions for treatment on behalf of their incapacitated loved ones, they are not allowed to do the opposite—to refuse life-sustaining treatment when they believe their loved one would not want it.

Eventually family and friends were able to collect and present enough evidence about Nancy Cruzan's statements and wishes before her accident to meet a "clear and convincing" legal standard that she would not want this life-sustaining treatment, given her persistent vegetative state. A Missouri court subsequently ruled that her feeding tube could then be removed, and she died quietly ten days later with her family by her side. If ever there were a strong argument for completing a formal advance directive, the ordeal of Nancy Cruzan and her family should be persuasive. It is also a powerful statement about how much our society is willing to override and compromise the rights and choices of dying persons and their families when they choose to forgo rather than continue life-sustaining medical treatment. The message for those who fear being kept alive by artificial measures under such conditions is clear: Let your wishes be clearly and explicitly known by formally selecting and informing a Health Care Proxy, or completing a Living Will.

The Supreme Court did not establish new standards for treatment refusal in the Cruzan decision, nor did it alter any state law. Surrogate decision makers (usually spouses or family members) for incompetent patients in most other states continue to make decisions on behalf of an incompetent patient by trying to reconstruct what the *patient would have wanted (substituted judgment), including the possibility of refusing artificial hydration and nutrition. In most states, a genuine attempt by the physician and the patient's surrogate decision maker to decide as they believe the patient would is the standard. "Clear and convincing" evidence in the form of a specific verbal statement or a written directive that covers the patient's condition is ideal when present. However, most incompetent patients have not made their wishes clear about specific procedures like feeding tubes. More commonly, at best one might find potentially ambiguous statements like not wanting to be "kept alive as a vegetable" or not wanting "heroic treatment" to guide treatment decisions. Such statements might be very valuable to a family member or friend trying to help make a decision on behalf of an incompetent patient whom they knew in many other ways, but might not meet a "clear and convincing" standard for treatment refusal as required in the state of Missouri. Thus, families in most states could recommend discontinuing feeding on behalf of a patient based in part on such prior statements, but in Missouri (and probably in New York) this would not be enough—the state would override the family's decisions because of the absence of explicit evidence.*

Precipitated in part by the Cruzan decision, the New York legislature passed the Health Care Proxy Act in 1990, which formally allowed its residents to select and empower an individual to make health-care decisions on their behalf in the event that they lose competence (the terms "proxy," "agent," and "surrogate" are synonymous, and often used interchangeably). The job of the person named to serve as a patient's Health Care Proxy is to make decisions as they believe the patient would, *using the patient's values and beliefs,* including the potential to refuse life-sustaining treatment. The New York State Task Force on Life and the Law recommended that the standard for all such decisions would be a genuine attempt to make the decision as the proxy believes the patient would, given knowledge about his or her current condition and prognosis (i.e., using substituted judgment). Unfortunately, discontinuing artificial nutrition and hydration was singled out in the final legislation by a special restrictive clause. In New York State, the Health Care Proxy selected by the patient can represent the patient to consent to or refuse any and all medical treatments, but must have "reasonable knowledge" of the patient's wishes about artificial hydration and nutrition in order to refuse it on his or her behalf. Sadly, we still have little guidance from the state about what constitutes "reasonable knowledge." Given our litigious and highly regulated medical environment, such ambiguous standards are likely to be interpreted very conservatively by physicians and health-care institutions.

In New York State, as in other parts of the country, many incompetent patients are being kept alive by artificial feeding simply because they never let their wishes about such practices be known. Such treatments are clearly justifiable when they have been specifically requested by the patient through an advance directive, or if the patient's surrogate decision maker has evidence that the patient would want to be kept alive in this manner. But the majority of incompetent patients simply never addressed the question, or else didn't articulate their wishes in a manner that meets these rigorous legal standards of proof. To understand the underlying decision-making process more fully, consider the following case that I came to know indirectly.

M R. A.

Mr. A. was an eighty-year-old man who had worked as a plumber for fifty-five years, finally retiring in his mid-seventies not because of any physical disability, but because he was becoming forgetful. Away from the work that had been the centerpiece of his life, he lacked direction and meaning. He began to drink too much alcohol, and spent most of his days in front of the television. When his wife died two years later, things began to unravel. He stopped eating regularly, became more and more confused, and stopped going out. With the support of his children and a community health nurse, he was able to stay at home for another year. Though not an introspective man by nature, he started to think more and more about death—wondering when it would come; thinking that it might not be any worse than this. He eventually developed trouble swallowing, and his weight loss and confusion accelerated. He was admitted to the hospital to see if any of his problems were reversible.

The medical workup for his memory loss unfortunately did not yield a treatable cause, and he was diagnosed with Alzheimer's Disease. His difficulty swallowing resulted from an associated deterioration of neuromuscular coordination. To see if the condition would improve with the correction of his nutritional problems, a tube was placed through his nose to put food and water directly into his stomach. Although formal informed consent was not solicited from his family, they were told that a feeding tube would be tried to see how he would respond. Mr. A. seemed to hate the tube in his nose and repeatedly pulled it out. After putting it back in several times, his arms were tied down in an effort to keep the tube in and to continue with the treatment trial. Like many restrained patients, Mr. A. was a master of escape, and began a battle of wills with the hospital staff around the clock.

Because Mr. A. was incompetent, his repeated verbal and nonverbal expressions that he didn't want a feeding tube were considered invalid. Though Mr. A. was clearly winning the battles, he eventually lost the war when a tube was surgically placed in his stomach positioned in such a way that he couldn't pull it out. His family gave consent for the surgical placement of the tube, but the choice they were offered was between continuing the battles over the tube through his nose or converting to a more comfortable tube directly

*into his stomach. There was little discussion about the overall pur-
pose and direction of treatment, or what Mr. A.'s wishes would have
been had he been able to decide for himself.*

*Mr. A. was eventually admitted to a nursing facility, where his
weight and nutrition stabilized with the daily tube feedings. His
dementia continued its relentless progression. Soon he did not even
recognize his children, and he had little meaningful interaction with
the staff. The family eventually accepted that he was not going to get
better, and asked their father's doctor if the feeding tube, which had
been initiated as a trial to see if he would improve, could be discontinued. In their discussions with Mr. A.'s doctor, they recalled what a
proud man he had been, how he had hated any sign of dependence
on others, how he had begun to look forward to death when he had
lived at home, and how all those who knew him felt strongly that he
would have hated living in his current condition. Unfortunately, as is
usually the case, no one could recall a specific statement by Mr. A. on
the actual subject of feeding tubes. Mr. A. did not worry about such
matters, and trusted he would be well taken care of when his time
came.*

*Mr. A.'s physician of many years agreed with the family that Mr.
A. would not want the tube feedings continued. But the nursing
facility had a policy that feeding tubes could not be discontinued
without a specific statement by the patient that he or she would not
want the tube—a policy developed on advice of legal council as an
attempt to minimize risk of State Health Department investigation
and of potential litigation. The legal council's primary job is to protect the institution from legal action and investigation, and the practical effects on patient care are often secondary. The nursing facility's
policy restricting the rights of incompetent patients or their surrogates to discontinue feeding tubes was not based on religious or
moral grounds, or on any strong sense that they were protecting
patients.*

*An ethics consultation was eventually obtained, and the State
Health Department was called to try to clarify its position with regard
to this case. A senior physician reviewer for the Health Department*

refused to give any advice about whether the data supporting the decision met its standards. Though he was unwilling either to get directly involved or to advise the consultant, the primary physician, or the nursing facility about how to proceed, he did guarantee that if anyone reported the case to the Department of Health after the removal of the feeding tube, a full investigation would follow to determine if the wishes of the patient were sufficiently known. This conversation handcuffed both the physician and the family, and the nursing facility continued to prohibit the removal of Mr. A.'s feeding tube. I want to reemphasize that there was agreement between Mr. A.'s family, his physician, the nursing facility administration, the nursing facility lawyer, and the ethics consultant that Mr. A.'s wishes and interests would be best served by taking out the feeding tube. The sole reason that the tube was to be left in was to prevent Health Department review, potential litigation, and adverse publicity.

After more extensive discussions, Mr. A. was eventually discharged from the nursing facility and admitted to an acute-care hospital, where his feeding tube was removed. He died quietly ten days later. The acute-care hospital felt that there was enough evidence about what Mr. A. would want to warrant taking a small risk on his behalf. The hospital's policy was that feeding tubes are like any other medical treatment that can be started and stopped depending on a thorough assessment of the benefits and burdens of treatment, and of the patient's wishes. Here the burdens of treatment were very high, and there was a consensus among those who cared about Mr. A. that he would want the feeding tube discontinued. The acute-care hospital took a small risk by putting the needs of an individual patient on a higher plane than the advice of risk managers. Unfortunately, too many health-care facilities err on the side of continued treatment where the incentives of minimizing legal risk are heavily weighted.

In New York State, and in many other parts of the country, incompetent patients who stop eating are being forced to receive artificial hydration and nutrition through feeding tubes, unless they have explicitly refused them in the past. In the absence of an explicit advance directive, institutions and legislatures are often overriding the substituted judgments of caring families who believe their loved one would not want to be kept alive in this manner. This occurs in spite of the fact that the vast majority of competent elderly patients, when surveyed about whether they would want tube feeding to prolong their life if they permanently lost mental competence, say they would not want it. The presumption that incompetent patients want this treatment unless they have specifically forbidden it in the past needs to be rethought, for the consequences are frightening. Until more sensible and representative policies are developed, the only way to protect one's future is to develop a personal philosophy about one's own wishes in the event that mental capacity is lost, and then express it formally in an advance directive.

Chapter 10

ADVANCE DIRECTIVES

Living Will or Health Care Proxy?

An advance directive is a formal document written by a competent person that is designed to guide medical treatment in the event of future mental incapacity. Without an advance directive, one runs the risk of having one's treatment guided more by the goals and values of the physician, the health-care institution, or the legislature than by one's own values and wishes. This can result in receiving unwanted life-prolonging treatment, or, conversely, in having potentially desired life-sustaining treatments arbitrarily withheld. The importance of executing an advance directive is enhanced even further by the passage of the Patient Self-Determination Act of 1990. This act requires that all U.S. hospitals, nursing facilities, health maintenance organizations, and other health-care delivery systems develop written policies regarding advance directives. Every patient who enters one of these organizations must be asked whether they have completed an advance directive, and they must be given information about the organization's related policies. Unfortunately, by the time people are admitted to an acute-care hospital or nursing facility, they may be too ill or too confused to consider such matters with the depth and seriousness that they require.

Clearly, the best time to consider an advance directive is *before* there is an acute, serious illness resulting in potential loss of mental capacity. Advance directives should be completed by all adult persons—from healthy young adults like Nancy Cruzan, who are not likely to have an immediate need, to the chronically ill retiree, like Mr. A., whose health and will to live is fading, and for whom difficult decisions about life-prolonging treatments are likely to be right around the corner. Such considerations must be moved out into the community, into doctors' offices, health fairs, church meetings, and lawyers' offices (though legal input is not necessary for a valid advance directive). This is potentially one of the most important decisions about health that a well person has to make.

LIVING WILL

A Living Will is a written advance directive in which competent people try to contemplate what medical interventions they would want should they lose mental capacity in the future. By specifying one's wishes in advance, even the strict "clear and convincing" legal standard would be met for the conditions and procedures covered. Unlike wills designed to distribute finances and property in the event of death, this will is "living" in the sense that it is activated when a person loses mental capacity but is still alive. Formal laws supporting the obligation of physicians to follow the directives set out in Living Wills exist in forty states, and there is a substantial body of case law to support the requirement that they be honored in other states.

There are two general types of Living Wills, each with advantages and disadvantages. The first defines a general philosophy of care that patients would want if they became incompetent under certain circumstances (i.e., terminal illness, dementia, persistent vegetative state). It is now clear that vague directives such as not wanting "heroic" or "extraordinary" treatments under these circumstances might protect a person from receiving unwanted cardiopulmonary resuscitation or perhaps mechanical ventilation, but when it comes to feeding tubes or other potentially life-prolonging treatments, the presumption to treat would probably prevail unless the treatments to be refused are specified. In order to try to anticipate all possibilities, a second very detailed form of Living Will lists a series of specific interventions that a person would or would not want if he or she becomes incompetent under several well-described circumstances.* These forms describe several patient scenarios in paragraph form, and then ask the respondent to check "yes" or "no" to a list of interventions of varying invasiveness and potential to prolong life. Checking "no" to an intervention would provide "clear and convincing" evidence that the treatment in question would be refused in the situation described.

Although these highly specific Living Wills help counteract some of the presumption that incompetent patients consent to treatment unless specifically stated otherwise, there remain two significant problems. First, it is not clear whether they apply to medical conditions that are similar to those described on the form but not exactly the same. The variations of illness associated with incompetence are myriad, so it would be impossible to anticipate and account for all possibilities. Even having executed such a document, there is no certainty it would meet the "clear and convincing" standard if one's condition differed significantly from those described. Secondly, the form forces respondents to make

*See "The Medical Directive" in the *Journal of the American Medical Association,* 1989;261:3288–93, for the best known example of this type of Living Will.

decisions in advance about highly technical interventions that they may know little about. Thus, patients might refuse treatments that would have enhanced their overall goals, and they might request treatments that interfere with their goals.

My preference in terms of Living Wills is for patients to specify their treatment goals and objectives under circumstances commonly associated with incompetence, including, but not necessarily restricted to, irreversible dementia, terminal illness, and persistent vegetative state. For example, a person who clearly wanted to avoid any and all life-prolonging treatments should he lose mental capacity might state in a Living Will: ". . . if I become terminally ill, permanently demented, or enter a persistent vegetative state, I want to die as quickly and comfortably as possible. In any such circumstance, I refuse any and all treatments that would be in any way life-prolonging. I would want only treatment intended to increase my comfort. I specifically refuse artificial hydration or nutrition of any kind should I develop any of these medical conditions, or any other conditions associated with permanent mental incapacity."

Another person might want to separate out Alzheimer's Disease, which has a more varied course and more potential for good quality of life. Such a person might use the above directive for terminal illness and persistent vegetative state, but state that "if I develop Alzheimer's Disease, I would like all noninvasive life-prolonging treatments such as antibiotics, fluids, and artificial nutrition as long as I still have the capacity for physical independence and meaningful interaction with my family, but I would not want extremely invasive treatments such as cardiopulmonary resuscitation, mechanical ventilation, or kidney dialysis. If I lose the capacity for physical independence or meaningful interaction with my family, I then only want treatments to enhance my comfort. I would then not want artificial hydration or nutrition."

A third person, with different goals and values, might use a Living Will to ensure that she is not arbitrarily excluded from any potentially effective life-prolonging treatment should she become mentally incompetent in the future. Such a person might state: ". . . should I become mentally incompetent for any reason, I still want to have any and all life-prolonging treatments that might be effective, including cardiopulmonary resuscitation. Under all circumstances, I would want to be artificially fed if I stop eating or drinking. I want to continue my fight for life even if the treatment appears to have significant burdens on me as a person."

These three examples were arbitrarily chosen to illustrate a range of directives. Each individual should tailor his or her Living Will to his/her own personal philosophy about potentially losing mental capacity in the future. The ideal advance directive is clear and direct about one's treatment goals and objectives, and specific about what types of existence one values and what one views as intolerable, so that physicians can continue to help incompetent persons meet their unique individual needs. Because of the controversy surrounding artificial hydration and nutrition, particularly in the states of New York and Missouri, I recommend that patients completing an advance directive make their wishes specifically known in this domain.

Patients admitted to our hospital choose one of three levels of care to guide treatment decisions:

1. *Critical care*—any and all life-sustaining measures, including extraordinary measures such as cardiopulmonary resuscitation, mechanical ventilation, and kidney dialysis;
2. *Conservative care*—treatment of all readily reversible medical conditions (antibiotics for infection, blood transfusion for anemia, etc.), but no extraordinary, invasive treatments (cardiopulmonary resuscitation, mechanical ventilation, kidney dialysis); or
3. *Comfort care*—treatment directed exclusively to relieving symptoms and alleviating suffering.

The Living Will forms included in the Appendix have been adapted to our hospital's "level of care" terminology. These forms can be copied and tailored for your personal use. Other equally effective forms should be available from your doctor, your local medical society, or from an organization called Choice in Dying (250 West 57th Street, New York, NY 10107; 212-246-6973). It is not necessary for a lawyer to assist or validate these forms in any way, though it may be useful to send your lawyer a copy of your completed form. Many lawyers have begun to include discussions of advance directives as an appropriate part of estate planning and the completion of a will.

HEALTH CARE PROXY

In the wake of the Cruzan case, several states have passed and many others are considering Health Care Proxy laws. By allowing competent persons to formally designate someone to help make decisions on their behalf should they lose mental capacity (a health care "proxy," "agent," or "surrogate"), such laws provide a powerful yet flexible vehicle to help ensure some control and limits on future medical decisions in the event of mental incapacity. The advantage of naming a proxy stems from the realization of the limitations of living wills—that it is impossible to anticipate all possible permutations of illness that might befall a person should they lose mental capacity. Severely ill persons who retain mental capacity can make decisions based on the specifics of their condition, in the context of their quality of life and the predicted effects of various interventions. In part because of the uncertainties that are inherent in medical prognostication and the intense emotions associated with the contemplation of death, such decisions are often difficult enough even for fully informed, competent people. To try to anticipate how one might respond to all possible future illnesses is nearly impossible. The Health Care Proxy can address the specifics of an incompetent patient's current medical condition, in light of her knowledge of the patient's health-care values and quality of life, and work with physicians to make decisions as she believes the patient would have wanted.

A well-informed Health Care Proxy is a tremendous asset to continuing medical decisions based on a genuine attempt to ascertain the patient's wishes. The job of the designated proxy is to help make informed decisions on the patient's behalf, *using the patient's values and beliefs,* not necessarily her own. It is therefore of utmost importance for the person who is formally selecting and naming a proxy to inform that proxy fully about her wishes should she become incompetent, and her attitudes toward life-sustaining treatment and death. It is vital to ensure that the proxy will make her best effort to use the patient's values to achieve the patient's goals rather than her own. If you have not thought deeply enough about the matters discussed in this book to have a personal philosophy about your own approach to the end of life, then you should have an extensive discussion with your potential Health Care Proxy to be sure that your goals and objectives in these difficult circumstances are eventually known. The Appendix shows a sample Health Care Proxy form that can be adapted for your use.

Under current law, a formally named Health Care Proxy has the flexibility to respond on your behalf to your specific medical situation with all its nuances and subtleties without necessarily being encumbered by a series of highly specific directives that could be taken out of context, as with some living wills. Some people have worried about potential conflicts between specific directives in Living Wills and the judgment of the Health Care Proxy on a given treatment for persons who have completed both documents. Though I suspect such conflicts will be rare, the safest course for those who want to complete both may be to keep the Living Will focused on general goals and objectives in common conditions associated with incompetence rather than specific treatments. The one exception is artificial hydration and nutrition. In some states, even a designated Health Care Proxy may be obstructed from refusing this treatment on behalf of an incompetent patient without demonstrating knowledge about the patient's specific wish. To ensure that decisions can continue to be made in this domain, a specific statement on both the Living Will and the Health Care Proxy forms is included here, so that feeding tubes and intravenous fluids can be either refused or withdrawn if that is what the patient would have wanted.

For those who have someone whom they can trust fully, the formal selection of a Health Care Proxy seems to be the best way at the present time to ensure that sensible decisions can continue to be made should one lose mental capacity in the future. A designated proxy has broad powers to participate in all medical decisions on behalf of the incompetent patient, both those that have been anticipated and those that haven't. Unfortunately, less than 10 percent of the population has completed a Living Will or formally selected someone to serve as their Health Care Proxy. With the passage of the Patient Self-Determination Act of 1990, as well as the tremendous publicity of recent "right to die" cases, it is difficult to believe that a person with strong views on the subject has not been made aware of the problem. In this context, it is going to be harder to argue against the "presumption" to treat incompetent persons who have not let their wishes be known. The incentive for completing an advance directive has never been higher for those who don't want invasive medical treatment if they become permanently mentally incompetent.

Why would a person who feared having his life medically prolonged not complete either a Living Will, or a Health Care Proxy, or both? The simplest answer is that although many people may be fascinated, fearful, or preoccupied by the possibility of suffering unnecessarily prior to death, it remains very difficult to think about death in personal terms. Although both my wife (who is my proxy) and I have very strong feelings and a clearly articulated vision about what we would want if either of us becomes incompetent, it took us three months to actually sign our proxy forms and have them witnessed. It was the same procrastination that delayed the completion of my first will—the possibility of my death seemed more real after I signed. For a very ill patient whose life is dwindling or for another person whose competence is slipping away, the completion of an advance directive is often the sad acknowledgment of an unwanted but inevitable future.

In addition to the fear of death and the grief that must accompany its acknowledgment, there are other barriers to this process. The forms and concepts of advance directives are rather difficult to understand and can be misinterpreted. For those with unquestioning faith in the benevolence of physicians, the need for such directives may mean coming to grips for the first time with medicine's true potential for harm as well as good. For those who are disenfranchised or discriminated against in other aspects of society, the opportunity to complete an advance directive may be viewed as a covert attempt by the hospital or the doctor to withhold effective treatment in order to contain costs. The selection of a Health Care Proxy can precipitate profound family conflict over who is to be appointed. These are just some of the main obstacles to completing advance directives. They begin to make it clear why so few have been formally completed, and why the absence of a signed advance directive cannot be equated with a presumption to consent to (or refuse) any treatment.

In New York State there is a hierarchy for surrogate decision makers who are empowered to make "do-not-resuscitate" decisions on behalf of incompetent patients. Rather than assuming that all incompetent patients who have not executed an advance directive want all possible medical treatments, why not assign them a Health Care Proxy using this same hierarchy? The highest person on this list who is willing to serve in this capacity, and who would clearly have the patient's interests at heart, would then be empowered to help make medical decisions using "substituted judgment." They would put themselves in the patient's shoes, and make decisions as they believe the patient would. Though it is acknowledged that substituted judgments are not 100 percent accurate, such action is certainly preferable to assuming that all incompetent patients who have not completed an advance directive want all life-sustaining treatments no matter what the benefits and burdens.

A word of clarification: an advance directive is definitely not the same as a "do-not-resuscitate" directive. As stated previously, an advance directive only goes into effect in the future, if a person loses competence; it says nothing about the kind of care that a person wants in the present or in the future if they remain competent and can be asked directly. The person who has completed an advance directive will continue to be offered all medical treatments applicable to their condition, which he or she can accept or reject, including cardiopulmonary resuscitation. If a competent person, because of his medical condition and the quality of his life in his present time, decides that he would not want cardiopulmonary resuscitation in the event he experiences a cardiac arrest, he must then complete a "do-not-resuscitate" document. Such documents cover only the specific treatment of cardiopulmonary resuscitation in the event of a cardiac arrest. Thus "do-not-resuscitate" documents cover only the potential present or future use of cardiopulmonary resuscitation, regardless of whether one is competent or incompetent. Advance directives (both Living Wills and Health Care Proxies) include a much broader range of medical decisions that take effect only in the future if the person loses mental capacity.

The 1988 California legislative initiative included the possibility of consenting to a physician-assisted death through an advance directive. I know of many persons who would want to take advantage of this option if it were legalized, and have expressed it in a "clear and convincing" way in their advance directive. Yet I have several insurmountable reservations about allowing physician-assisted death by advance directive. First of all, I am unsure how one would decide about the moment of death under such a system. Since the person can no longer tell you whether they would rather die today or next month, how is the final decision to be made? The timing of the event would necessarily be influenced by factors other than the wishes of the patient. Secondly, a competent person has the option of changing his or her mind all the way up to the event. There is no way to guarantee that the incompetent person would not change her mind about this final act if she had full knowledge of her condition. Finally, it will be difficult if not impossible to prove that severe, unrelenting suffering is continuing in the face of comfort care. Though this might be inferred based on past statements and observations of the patient while receiving comfort care, the patient could not possibly validate these subjective assessments. The potential for misinterpretation and abuse in such advance directives is simply too great.

Though I have unresolvable reservations about offering physician-assisted death to incompetent patients who have requested it through their advance directives, I believe that we must respond to the plight of those who have clearly let it be known that they do not want to live under such conditions. As physicians we could do this by treating them as conservatively as possible, avoiding all life-extending treatment, and doing everything within our power to minimize their discomfort, maximize their dignity, and facilitate an easy death. For those who have expressed such wishes in their advance directive, all treatments in all settings would be directed exclusively toward enhancing comfort and dignity, and explicitly not to prolonging life. The goal would be to make death as humane, dignified, and easy as possible, using medical intervention to ease the way but not choose the moment.

BRAD

Brad was a thirty-five-year-old man with a severe neuromuscular disorder which he inherited from his father. He had struggled for all that he had achieved in life. Nothing had come easily. He had been told that he would never walk, yet he eventually learned to get around his disability and walk with a gait that was most unusual, but got him where he wanted to go. He was thought to be retarded as a child, but this misconception was based more on his physical disability than any lack of mental acuity. He made up for lost time, and eventually was able to complete a college education. His movements and physique were unique, but perhaps his most striking feature was a remarkable collection of tattoos of powerful animals scattered over his arms and chest.

Brad was a loner. He did not trust people readily, and doctors were people that he depended on only warily, out of necessity rather than want. Brad and I were just beginning to get to know and trust one another when he began to develop some unusual infections that heralded the diagnosis of acquired immunodeficiency syndrome (AIDS). The diagnosis for him was not a surprise, and it represented another cross to bear and fight against with all his considerable inner resources. He started the usual treatments to fight the virus and to prevent infections, but unfortunately these had an unusual side effect which made his already damaged muscles much weaker. The medicine was changed, but his loss of strength persisted. He had to spend more and more time in a wheelchair—a loss that I thought might have overwhelmed him, but which he confronted with remarkable determination and creativity.

Brad stabilized for several months and was even beginning to regain his strength when he had the first of a series of pulmonary infections that necessitated hospitalization. He hated the hospital, and each time he was admitted there was a struggle with the staff over control that usually centered on whether or not he could smoke *in his room (in our "smoke-free" hospital). Because he disliked being in the hospital so much, and because his prognosis was very poor, Brad and I began to discuss his wishes with regard to cardiopulmonary resuscitation and other life-sustaining measures. Like most persons with advanced AIDS, Brad had two potential dilemmas that he might have to face. The first was the possibility of a long period on a breathing machine because of recurrent lung infections with pneumocystis carini. Brad was particularly vulnerable to this because of his underlying neuromuscular disorder and limited chest muscle strength. The second was the potential for AIDS dementia, which is a deterioration of the brain that can occur through a variety of mechanisms.*

Brad was terrified about the potential for dependence on medical technology in his future, yet for now he still wanted to use all medical measures to vigorously fight for life. If he became demented or permanently dependent on a breathing machine, he wanted a promise that all life-sustaining treatment would be stopped and that he would be allowed to die. We therefore discussed his completing an advance directive to allow decision making to continue in accordance with his wishes should he lose competence, but did not complete a "do-not-resuscitate" document because he wanted to give that treatment a try if it had any potential of working. Brad did not have any close friends or family members he trusted enough to designate as his Health Care Proxy, but a church person he came to know consented to serve in that capacity. They had several talks about Brad's values and wishes, after which the forms were completed.

Two months later, after returning from a long-anticipated trip to New York City, Brad had a precipitous decline in mental function. He was admitted to the hospital, where an aggressive medical evaluation showed that his brain had begun a process of rapid deterioration that was not treatable. Within a week, Brad became sleepy, confused, then unarousable. Because he had lost competence and the loss was irreversible, his Health Care Proxy was contacted to try to make some decisions about the direction of his care. After discussing the deteriorating medical situation with his proxy, we agreed that Brad would no longer want aggressive medical treatment, given the current state of his disease and its prognosis. We also agreed to use the philosophy of comfort care, and to discontinue all treatments that were not clearly directed to his comfort and dignity. Since cardiopulmonary resuscitation would now be meaningless, given the agreed-upon goal of comfort care, Brad's proxy consented to my issuing a "do-not-resuscitate" order. In making these decisions, both Brad's proxy and I felt that we were acting in accordance with Brad's previously stated wishes.

Brad went into a deep sleep. His agitation was treated with a combination of narcotics and sedatives. Though he was too sick to acknowledge their presence, several friends and the clergyperson sat in a constant vigil so that someone would be there should he momentarily awaken.

Brad died quietly two days later in the presence of friends. His life had always been a struggle and his last months were no different. Yet Brad was allowed to die in relative comfort in the company of friends after waging a heroic fight, first against his neuromuscular disease and then against AIDS. Though Brad had been dealt a difficult hand, he lived as fully as possible within the confines of a flawed body that was finally overcome by the ravages of a deadly virus. Brad lived and then died with dignity, after a lifelong battle which he himself defined and in many ways won.

Chapter 11

CHALLENGES AND FINAL THOUGHTS

Balancing a reverence for life with a belief that death should come with dignity and peace is the challenge posed by each of the individuals whose stories weave throughout this book. In spite of the areas of controversy, there is broad agreement among physicians, ethicists, and policy makers about the rights of patients to refuse treatment, about the need for better and broader application of comfort care for the dying, and finally about the potential effectiveness of advance directives (Health Care Proxies and Living Wills) to help ensure that the medical decisions made for incompetent patients continue to be based on their wishes and values.

The possibility of severe suffering at the end of life is now more openly acknowledged, as are the potentials and limitations of currently permitted options. This acknowledgment provides hope for those who have witnessed someone they love struggle before death, yet there remains considerable controversy about how the medical profession or society should respond to the compelling challenge posed by those for whom death provides the only escape from severe suffering. I hope that an understanding of this dilemma has been made more personal by considering the ideas and stories presented here.

In this last chapter, I want to pose a series of deceptively simple challenges to patients, doctors, institutions, and policy makers. Although each of us is potentially a patient who must someday face our own death, the other groups must address distinct but overlapping challenges.

THE CHALLENGE TO PATIENTS

1. *Develop a personal philosophy:* Entertaining the inevitability of one's own death is not an easy task. Most of us wish we could live forever, and there is a subtle but significant injury to our sense of omnipotence that comes when we accept that we can't. Yet without having thoroughly considered what we would want should we be unfortunate enough to become very sick or debilitated in the future, we may have to come to grips with medicine's limitations for the first time just when we wish it were most powerful. Should we lose the competence to make decisions before we have developed our own philosophy, we unwittingly may forfeit the potential for exerting any control over the final stages of our life.

One way to help develop a coherent personal philosophy is to learn about the deaths of people in your family and of your closest friends. By sharing stories of the deaths of people we care about, the process can be demystified, and we can begin to understand in more personal terms the many faces death can have. What does it mean to you to have a "good death"? Are there aspects of dying that would deprive it of personal meaning? What are your biggest fears about death? What would be most important to you at the end?

One may find significant, sometimes painful family secrets in exploring these stories. Yet they contain some of the key elements to a deeper understanding of life and death, and out of them may emerge a personal philosophy that can guide you or those taking care of you in the event of future illness.

2. *Complete an advance directive:* Though I personally favor the Health Care Proxy over the Living Will because of its increased flexibility, either type of advance directive will allow you to maintain some control over medical decisions should you lose mental capacity in the future. Since the job of the Health Care Proxy is to continue to make decisions according to your personal philosophy about death, it is critical that your beliefs and wishes be clearly developed and communicated. Empowering a person to make such decisions on your behalf without providing her with clear directions places an unfair burden on her if she is faced with *your* life-and-death decisions. Thus, developing your end-of-life philosophy and then expressing it clearly are inextricably interwoven parts of an advance directive. Once your proxy is fully informed of your wishes, it is also important to ensure that she will be assertive on your behalf. The pressures to continue life-prolonging treatment will need the counterbalancing, well-articulated force of the patient's wishes if the possibility of alternative treatments is to be seriously entertained.

Unless you complete a formal advance directive document while mentally competent, it is likely that you will continue to receive potent life-prolonging medical treatments if you become incompetent, even if the quality of your life becomes very poor. Once you have completed your own advance directive, encourage your parents, siblings, children, and friends to do the same. The stakes can be very high.

3. *Talk with your doctor about your advance directive:* This conversation serves several functions. First, it ensures that your doc-

tor will honor your wishes and not override them if you become incompetent. Though it might seem frightening, doctors (like all other groups of people) vary considerably in their approach to end-of-life decisions and in their willingness to let patients die. If your doctor's philosophy about death differs substantially from your own, then it is important that you know about it now, while you are competent to discuss how future decisions will be made. If you lose competence and have not let your philosophy be known, then it is likely that your doctor's values and beliefs rather than your own will be the driving force.

Second, ask your doctor to tell the complete truth about your prognosis should you get sick in the future, including the possibility and odds of death. This does not necessarily mean that you will want to stop active treatment, or that you should give up hope for recovery. But it does allow the possibility of comfort care to be entertained at an earlier stage in your illness, not just when death is imminent and all possible medical treatments have been exhausted. It also allows you time to make contingency plans with your family in case death comes sooner rather than later.

Finally, particularly if you are seriously ill, learn if your doctor can talk openly about death, and if she will make a commitment to work with you no matter where the illness may take you. If you are fearful about the possibility of undue suffering during the final stages of a terminal illness, let your doctor know, and gain assurance that she will do everything in her power to minimize it. If the physician will not acknowledge death or suffering as a possibility, then I would challenge them with your beliefs and experiences. Hopefully this conversation will initiate a deeper understanding and bond on which future decisions can be based. If your physician can understand and respect your wishes, and can make this kind of commitment, you are well on your way to ensuring yourself a dignified death.

4. *Become politically active:* The main force for changing the restrictions on physician-assisted death will come not from the

medical profession but rather from the general public. It is very important for witnesses to keep sharing their experiences, since the tragedy of the unrelieved suffering of dying patients is much more fully acknowledged by the medical profession as a result of these compelling stories. With that acknowledgment comes the possibility of a change in public policy and legal restrictions. Although I personally favor such changes, I believe that they should be approached very carefully. We need safeguards that will minimize abuse but not prove so overly restrictive that suffering patients cannot find an escape. If such changes do occur, we must carefully monitor their effects to ensure that the benefits outweigh the burdens.

THE CHALLENGE TO DOCTORS

1. *Acknowledge and try to alleviate end-of-life suffering:* Although physicians are clearly agents of life, they also have a major role in caring for patients who are dying. A doctor's top priorities in providing traditional medical care are to treat the underlying disease and to prolong life. Sometimes we ask people to tolerate considerable suffering in order to achieve these goals. When treating a person who is dying, the aims of minimizing suffering, maintaining patient choice and control, and alleviating symptoms should take priority over traditional medical concerns. Comfort care is a well-defined strategy for achieving these ends. Unfortunately, doctors vary considerably in their knowledge and skill at providing comfort care. Clearly we professionals must do a better job of learning about and delivering this more humane approach to the care of the dying. Comfort care, carefully and creatively applied, can help most patients achieve a dignified, relatively comfortable death.

2. *Encourage the completion of advance directives:* It always surprises me to learn how many physicians have not completed advance directives for themselves—even those who have seen what can happen and clearly don't want to continue aggressive medical treatments should they become incompetent. Many doctors remain uncomfortable with contemplating and openly discussing death, either their own or their patients'. Yet we are in a unique position to facilitate the completion of advance directives by our patients. As physicians, I believe that we must go through the hard process of defining our own personal philosophies and then articulating them in advance directives. Once we have personally completed this process, we are in a better position to help initiate and facilitate it for our patients. If this leads to a more open discussion about medicine's limitations as well as its potential, then we will all benefit from this more realistic understanding.

3. *Never abandon the dying:* Just as we would never walk away from a patient who was having difficulty in the middle of surgery, we must never abandon patients who develop complex problems in the process of dying. The fight against disease often brings out heroic efforts by physicians on behalf of their patients. Their caring and effort to find creative solutions seem to know no bounds. Many times the dying, as they face the unknown of death and the ravages of the last stages of their illness, need that same intensive caring and creativity. Since there are no clear formulas for how to approach these problems, physicians must maintain a sharp mind and an open heart.

When intensively applied comfort care is not working well and the patient expresses a wish to die, this wish needs open exploration. If the wish to die includes a request for assisted death, the physician must first fully understand the request, and make sure it is not a cry for help that can be dealt with within the traditional guidelines of comfort care. Assuming that the request is rational, and all acceptable methods of comfort care have been exhausted, then the physician must look inward to her own values, in the context of existing legal and professional risks, to decide how to respond. If the physician decides that she cannot respond to the patient's request for assisted death, together they must continue to search for alternatives that can somehow improve the patient's plight. Turning down the request should in no way stop the discussion, nor does it mean that the intensive search for acceptable alternatives should cease.

4. *Define acceptable options for the treatment of patients with intolerable suffering.* I don't think there is much debate among experienced clinicians about whether severe suffering sometimes exists in the face of comfort care. The question is what alternatives should be made available, and what is the appropriate role for physicians. Physicians are deeply divided on these issues. A majority in most surveys favor opening up the possibility of their more active involvement in facilitating a humane death, yet not all those in favor said they would be willing to become directly involved themselves. We as physicians have to think carefully about what it would mean to us personally and professionally to get directly involved in aiding severely suffering patients to die. If we decide as individuals or as a profession that we cannot assist our patients in this way, then we must be much more clear and open about the limits and potential of what we can do when it is clear that death will provide the only relief. Answers will not come easily, but that is no reason to avoid the questions.

THE CHALLENGE TO INSTITUTIONS

1. Make the translation from policy to practice as simple and straightforward as possible. Health policy and legislation often emerges using very complex, legalistic terminology that is unwieldy when transferred directly into practice. Health care proxy documents, for example, vary from simple one-page forms (such as the one in the appendix) to multipaged, single-spaced legal briefs. The drafters of legislation and policy intend to provide a framework within which practical decision making can occur. Doctors, patients, lawyers, and policy makers must cooperate to construct understandable, easy-to-use documents to record "do-not-resuscitate," Health Care Proxy, and Living Will decisions to ensure that these facilitate rather than impede sensible decision making. Periodically these documents should be reviewed, clarified, and simplified if appropriate. Important documents such as advance directives also need to be translated into other languages, and to be made more accessible to people from different cultures.

Similarly, it is possible to comply with the letter of the law without carrying out its intent. For example, the Patient Self-Determination Act of 1990 requires that all patients entering a health-care facility be asked whether they have completed an advance directive, and be offered relevant written information. Compliance with the law can be achieved by having a clerk ask this one additional question in the admitting process, recording the answer, and handing the patient several additional forms in the packet of admitting information. This is unlikely to initiate the complex and important dialogue that is required to complete an advance directive in an informed way. If institutions truly believe that advance directives will help them provide better care should a patient lose competence, then they should promote a serious discussion between patients, their families, and their physicians.

2. *Risk management must be balanced by patient advocacy.* Health-care facilities are legitimately fearful of litigation and review. As a result, "risk management" has been elevated to a major institutional objective, sometimes taking precedence over good patient care. A legal consultant may advise a health-care institution to continue life-sustaining treatment when there is any uncertainty about a person's wishes, even if the preponderance of evidence suggests that the person would not want the treatment, and family and physician agree. There is little institutional risk in continuing aggressive, life-prolonging treatments for incompetent patients overriding the wishes of caring families, unless the patient has made his refusal unequivocally clear through an advance directive. Some institutions are forcing incompetent patients to continue the use of feeding tubes against their family's wishes not because of patient advocacy, but because of fear of review or litigation. If legal consultants and other risk managers find that good care must be compromised to minimize institutional risk, then they need to make this fact known publicly both to the people being admitted to their facility, and to the legislators and reviewers who have generated these well-intended but ultimately harmful policies. It is only by increasing public awareness of the forces impinging on health-care decisions that a policy can eventually evolve that will protect patients from unwanted treatments and unwarranted exclusions.

THE CHALLENGE TO POLICY MAKERS

1. *Acknowledge the problem of intolerable end-of-life suffering:* Much of the debate about whether or not to allow physician-assisted death under defined circumstances has been clouded by

the implication that perhaps the problem doesn't exist. Intolerable suffering is suggested to be the result of inadequate physician skill or of a lack of access to comfort care. Limited access to health care in general and hospice care in specific, as well as lack of physician experience providing comfort care, remain potentially reversible problems that can result in unnecessary suffering. Though these social and political problems deserve our utmost attention, they should not be merged with the dilemma faced by incurably ill patients who are suffering in spite of often heroic efforts by physicians, other health-care providers, and families to provide comfort. These tragic cases are not common, but they are certainly not rare. The first step in addressing the problem at the policy level is to acknowledge that it exists, and that we don't have adequate solutions, given the current legal and professional restraints. The lack of acknowledgment in some circles has frightened many people who have witnessed such agonizing deaths firsthand—how can we hope to address a health policy problem that we pretend doesn't exist?

2. *Don't argue over positions:* We must learn from and not repeat the abortion debate, in which followers are forced to make a decision between being pro-life and pro-choice. There must be some middle ground where we can maintain our reverence for life, while at the same time acknowledging the possibility of intolerable suffering before death and the need for those experiencing it to have a wider range of choices. Inflammatory rhetoric about doctors killing their patients does not promote understanding of the complex issues involved in potentially taking on a compassionate role in physician-assisted suicide. Conversely, images about widespread end-of-life suffering and abandonment do not help the uninitiated appreciate the genuine effectiveness of intensive comfort care for the dying. A responsible middle ground is possible if we keep the needs of dying patients foremost in our minds and our political agendas in the background.

3. Openly acknowledge the risks and benefits of competing strategies: There is no risk-free way to proceed by either prohibiting or allowing physician-assisted suicide. Clearly defined safeguards can minimize the risk of subtle coercion or even abuse, but there is no way to guarantee that this cannot occur on rare occasions even with the most conservatively drafted policy. Similarly, there are substantial risks to maintaining the current prohibitions—including the potential for abandoning patients before death, for exaggerating the already immense power differences between doctors and their dying patients, and for secrecy, risk taking, and idiosyncratic practice for those doctors who do choose to assist. The benefits of moving forward are clear to those who are suffering intolerably with no escape other than death, as well as to those who would be reassured by the possibility of such an option even if unexercised. Similarly, the benefits of holding on to current restrictions include the maintenance of long-standing professional and religious prohibitions that have traditionally served us well, lessening the risk of involuntary euthanasia, and encouraging the development of creative alternatives that fall short of physician-assisted suicide.

No matter which way the public debate proceeds, we need more careful analysis and understanding of the effects of public policy on real patients. Public policy guiding the care of the dying must become more responsive to the values and needs of incurably ill persons who have so little to gain and so much to lose. The safeguards and criteria proposed in Chapter 8 might serve as a starting point for this debate. What is to be lost by allowing competent patients who have exhausted all acceptable comfort-oriented measures the possibility of a quick, painless, and controlled death? If we decide to maintain the current prohibitions, we must have clearly articulated, convincing reasons for depriving such people of the possibility of a more dignified death.

THE CHALLENGE POSED BY
STEWART A. KING, M. D.

This letter was written to the editor of the *New England Journal of Medicine* in response to my original article about Diane, presented in the preface:

I am a retired general surgeon essentially quadriplegic [cannot move his arms or legs] and dependent on a respirator because of advanced amyotrophic lateral sclerosis [an incurable, progressive neuromuscular disease commonly known as Lou Gehrig's disease]. . . .

Who better than the individual patient can decide when the burdens that illness imposes on oneself, one's family, and society can no longer be justified by any possible contribution to the well-being of anyone? Transient extremes of depression are correctly resisted by all; nonetheless, to the patient, there has to be an acceptable reason for carrying on.

Of course I agree that the decision to seek death must be challenged by the medical profession and the family, but if no valid rationale can be offered for sustained existence, what then? Can the profession justify simply walking away from the problem? I think not.

Why should a spouse or a child or a dedicated health professional be subjected to the threat of a legal proceeding for easing the suffering of a desperately ill person who consciously and rationally asks that the anguish be ended?

When my continued survival is no longer meaningful (to me), I hope that a caring physician will make the transition as easy as possible. I realize that some health professionals will find it impossible to do this, but I hope that they and society will understand the true compassion for their patients' suffering that motivates the physicians who do help those in need. And I would hope that this understanding will lead to the elimination of unwarranted legal constraints when patient, family, and physician all concur.

SOME FINAL THOUGHTS

I have reflected extensively about the care that I gave to Diane over those three months, and the case I presented in the *New England Journal of Medicine* has been thoroughly dissected and analyzed. I firmly believe that the possibility of a controlled death gave Diane the freedom to live those final months without being haunted by fear that she would linger in a dependent, debilitated state prior to death. In her eyes, such an existence would have been worse than death, and she would likely have found some way to avoid it even without my help. In the face of being afflicted with acute leukemia, Diane took charge and made active decisions that helped to control her fate in a way that had meaning and purpose for her. Her course was not easy, and it might not have been chosen by many other people, but it was completely consistent with her carefully thought out personal values and beliefs. At the end, Diane was less afraid of death than she was of dependency and progressive debility. Though she did not wish for death, for her it became the lesser of two unfortunate evils. Diane did not ask to become ill or to face these difficult choices, but she did ask to be allowed to control her destiny in a way that she found dignified and acceptable.

My biggest regret about the care that I gave Diane was that she died alone. Though she did this of her own free will, her choice was colored by her knowledge of current laws prohibiting assisted suicide. By being alone at her death, she could feel secure that neither her family nor I would be successfully prosecuted should her act be discovered. Diane had made fully informed, very thoughtful decisions at each stage of her illness. She had high-quality time with her family and friends, and showed how a mature, thoughtful person can face the inevitability of death with grace, humor, control, and dignity. She even risked getting an infection that could have shortened her life further to meet with a large group of our students, residents, and staff in a conference devoted to a patient's right to refuse treatment. The participants in that conference learned in an unforgettable way what informed consent—and refusal—is all about. Diane was a thoughtful, challenging, loving, very generous person, who had the courage to take charge of her own destiny. She should not have had to pay for taking charge by feeling forced to die alone.

As to my own personal philosophy about death, I cherish life and do not want to die. At this point in my life, I would be willing to fight substantial medical battles to continue living. But for me, continued living must always have a purpose. I hope that I will be willing to struggle to find enough new meaning and direction to keep going should I become severely ill and debilitated in the future. But if and when that struggle comes to an end and no meaning can be found or recovered, take the bed to the window and let me fly as quickly and painlessly as possible. If there is a next life, I hope it is as challenging, interesting, and filled with love and heartache as this one has been. If not, then at least there will be peace and relief.

APPENDIX

Advance Directives

1
DEFINITIONS (p. 219)

2
QUESTIONS AND ANSWERS (p. 221)

3
SAMPLE FORMS (p. 229)

ADVANCE DIRECTIVES

1) Definitions

You can make decisions and issue directives *now* that will ensure that your wishes are followed in the event you become incapable of making important decisions about the medical care you receive.

This appendix contains the documents listed below along with guidelines on the Health Care Proxy.

Please read each document carefully and discuss them with your family, doctor, and close friends.

Living Will

This document addresses your wishes regarding extraordinary life-sustaining treatment. It provides instructions about the health care treatment you want or do not want provided in the event that you are unable to make these decisions.

It is our hospital policy to follow the wishes you have expressed in a properly executed Advance Directive.

Health Care Proxy

This document allows you to choose someone you trust to make treatment decisions for you in the event that you are unable to do so. By designating a "Health Care Agent" who knows your wishes, your treatment can be provided accordingly.

Advance Directive for Artificial Nutrition and Hydration

This allows you to document now whether you want feeding tubes for nutrition and hydration if you are permanently unconscious or have a terminal illness or condition in which you would not want your life unreasonably prolonged. Only you can make this decision, according to New York State law. This Directive document is included on both the Health Care Proxy and the Living Will.

What to Do with the Forms

1. If you are being admitted to the hospital or are having ambulatory surgery, bring the completed forms with you to the admitting office.
2. Be sure to send copies of the forms to your doctor(s), the agent you appointed, family members or close friends, your hospital and your lawyer.

2) Questions and Answers*

What is a Health Care Proxy?

A new law, called the New York Health Care Proxy law, allows you to appoint someone you trust—for example, a family member or close friend—to decide about treatment if you lose the ability to decide for yourself. You can appoint someone by signing a form called a Health Care Proxy.

You can give the person you select, your "health care agent," as little or as much authority as you want. You can allow your health care agent to decide about all health care or only about certain treatments. You may also give your agent instructions that he or she has to follow. Your agent can then make sure that health care professionals follow your wishes and can decide how your wishes apply as your medical condition changes. Hospitals, doctors, and other health care providers must follow your agent's decisions as if they were your own.

*The information on these pages has been provided by the New York State Department of Health.

Why should I choose a health care agent?

If you become too sick to make health care decisions, someone else must decide for you. Health care professionals often look to family members for guidance. But family members are not allowed to decide to stop treatment, even when they believe that is what you would choose or what is best for you under the circumstances. Appointing an agent lets you control your medical treatment by:

- allowing your agent to stop treatment when he or she decides that is what you would want or what is best for you under the circumstances;
- choosing one family member to decide about treatment because you think that person would make the best decisions or because you want to avoid conflict or confusion about who should decide; and
- choosing someone outside your family to decide about treatment because no one in your family is available or because you prefer that someone other than a family member decide about your health care.

How can I appoint a health care agent?

All competent adults can appoint a health care agent by signing a form called a Health Care Proxy. You don't need a lawyer, just two adult witnesses. You can use the form printed here, but you don't have to.

When would my health care agent begin to make treatment decisions for me?

Your health care agent would begin to make treatment decisions after doctors decide that you are not able to make treatment decisions. As long as you are able to make treatment decisions for yourself, you will have the right to do so.

What decisions can my health care agent make?

Unless you limit your health care agent's authority, your agent will be able to make any treatment decision that you could have made if you were able to decide for yourself. Your agent can agree that you should receive treatment, choose among different treatments, and decide that treatments should not be provided, in accord with your wishes and interests. If your health care agent is not aware of your wishes about artificial nutrition and hydration (nourishment and water provided by feeding tubes), he or she will not be able to make decisions about these measures. Artificial nutrition and hydration are used in many circumstances, and are often used to continue the life of patients who are in a permanent coma.

How can I give my agent written instructions?

See "Filling Out the Proxy Form" below.

How will my health care agent make decisions?

You can write instructions on the proxy form. Your agent must follow your oral and written instructions, as well as your moral and religious beliefs. If your agent does not know your wishes or beliefs, your agent is legally required to act in your best interests.

Who will pay attention to my agent?

All hospitals, doctors and other health care facilities are legally required to obey the decisions by your agent. If a hospital objects to some treatment options (such as removing certain treatment) they must tell you or your agent IN ADVANCE.

What if my health care agent is not available when decisions must be made?

You can appoint an alternate agent to decide for you if your health care agent is not available or able to act when decisions must be made. Otherwise, health care providers will make treatment decisions for you that follow instructions you gave while you were still able to do so. Any instructions that you write on your Health Care Proxy form will guide health care providers under these circumstances.

What if I change my mind?

It is easy to cancel the proxy, to change the person you have chosen as your health care agent, or to change any treatment instructions you have written on your Health Care Proxy form. Just fill out a new form. In addition, you can require that the Health Care Proxy expire on a specified date or if certain events occur. Otherwise, the Health Care Proxy will be valid indefinitely. If you choose your spouse as your health care agent and you get divorced or legally separated, the proxy is automatically cancelled.

Can my health care agent be legally liable for decisions made on my behalf?

No. Your health care agent will not be liable for treatment decisions made in good faith on your behalf. Also, he or she cannot be held liable for costs of your care, just because he or she is your agent.

Is a Health Care Proxy the same as a Living Will?

No. A Living Will is a document that provides specific instructions about health care treatment. It is generally used to declare wishes to refuse life-sustaining treatment under certain circumstances.

In contrast, the Health Care Proxy allows you to choose someone you trust to make treatment decisions on your behalf. Unlike a Living Will, a Health Care Proxy does not require that you know in advance all the decisions that may arise. Instead, your health care agent can interpret your wishes as medical circumstances change and can make decisions you could not have known would have to be made. The Health Care Proxy is just as useful for decisions to receive treatment as it is for decisions to stop treatment. If you complete a Health Care Proxy form, but also have a Living Will, the Living Will provides instructions for your health care agent, and will guide his or her decisions.

Where should I keep the proxy form after it is signed? Give a copy to your agent, your doctor, and any other family members or close friends you want. You can also keep a copy in your wallet or purse or with other important papers.

Appointing a health care agent is a serious decision. Make sure you talk about it with your family, close friends and your doctor. Do it in advance, not just when you are planning to enter the hospital.

About the Health Care Proxy

This is an important legal form. Before signing this form, you should understand the following facts:

1. This form gives the person you choose as your agent the authority to make all health care decisions for you, except to the extent you say otherwise in this form. "Health care" means any treatment, service or procedure to diagnose or treat your physical or mental condition.

2. Unless you say otherwise, your agent will be allowed to make all health care decisions for you, including decisions to remove or withhold life-sustaining treatment.

3. Unless your agent knows your wishes about artificial nutrition and hydration (nourishment and water provided by a feeding tube), he or she will not be allowed to refuse those measures for you.

4. Your agent will start making decisions for you when doctors decide that you are not able to make health care decisions for yourself.

You may write on this form any information about treatment that you do not desire and/or those treatments that you want to make sure you receive. Your agent must follow your instructions (oral and written) when making decisions for you.

If you want to give your agent written instructions, do so right on the form. For example, you could say:

- If I become terminally ill, I do/don't want to receive the following treatments . . .
- If I am in a coma or unconscious, with no hope of recovery, then I do/don't want . . .
- If I have brain damage or a brain disease that makes me unable to recognize people or speak and there is no hope that my condition will improve, I do/don't want . . .

Examples of medical treatments about which you may wish to give your agent special instructions are listed below. This is **not** a complete list of the treatments about which you may leave instructions.

- artificial respiration
- artificial nutrition and hydration (nourishment and water provided by feeding tube)
- cardiopulmonary resuscitation (CPR)
- dialysis
- Blood transfusions
- antibiotics

Talk about choosing an agent with your family and/or close friends. You should discuss this form with a doctor or another health care professional, such as a nurse or social worker, before you sign it to make sure that you understand the types of decisions that may be made for you. You may also wish to give your doctor a signed copy. You do **not** need a lawyer to fill out this form.

You can choose any adult (over 18), including a family member, or close friend, to be your agent. If you select a doctor as your agent, he or she may have to choose between acting as your agent or as your attending doctor; a physician cannot do both at the same time. Also, if you are a patient or resident of a hospital, nursing home or mental hygiene facility, there are special restrictions about naming someone who works for that facility as your agent. You should ask staff at the facility to explain those restrictions.

You should tell the person you choose that he or she will be your health care agent. You should discuss your health care wishes and this form with your agent. Be sure to give him or her a signed copy. Your agent cannot be sued for health care decisions made in good faith.

Even after you have signed this form, you have the right to make health care decisions for yourself as long as you are able to do so, and treatment cannot be given to you or stopped if you object. You can cancel the control given to your agent by telling him or her or your health care provider orally or in writing.

Filling Out the Proxy Form

1. Write your name and the name, home address and telephone number of the person you are selecting as your agent.

2. If you have special instructions for your agent, you should write them here. Also if you wish to limit your agent's authority in any way, you should say so here. If you do not state any limitations, your agent will be allowed to make all health care decisions that you could have made, including the decision to consent to or refuse life-sustaining treatment.

3. You may write the name, home address and telephone number of an alternate agent.

4. This form will remain valid indefinitely unless you set an expiration date or condition for its expiration. This section is optional and should be filled in only if you want the health care proxy to expire.

5. You must date and sign the proxy. If you are unable to sign

yourself, you may direct someone else to sign in your presence. Be sure to include your address.

Two witnesses at least 18 years of age must sign your proxy. The person who is appointed agent or alternate agent cannot sign as a witness.

3)
Sample Forms

LIVING WILL

To: My Family, my Physicians, my Lawyer, any Medical Facility in whose care I happen to be, any Individual who may become responsible for my Health Affairs, and All Others Whom It May Concern:

I, being of sound mind and over 18 years of age, hereby issue a directive, which I intend to be legally binding, **which shall become effective at some future time, only under the following circumstances:**

1. When I become unable to make my own decisions or express my wishes; *AND*

2. CHOOSE ALL THAT YOU WANT TO APPLY

☐ If I have a terminal illness; and/or

☐ I am permanently unconscious; and/or

☐ If extraordinary life support procedures or "heroic measures" would be medically futile; and/or

☐ Under the following circumstances (Please specify, for example, dementia, severe neurological illness or other permanent disabling condition to which you want this Directive to apply):

_____

_____

_____

_____

Then I direct that my dying not be unreasonably prolonged; *AND*

CHOOSE *ONE*

☐ I wish to have COMFORT CARE ONLY, which is directed only toward relieving pain and suffering, regardless of the progress of my disease.

☐ I want CONSERVATIVE CARE, which is usual treatment (such as antibiotics) *but not* extraordinary treatment (such as cardiopulmonary resuscitation, mechanical ventilation, kidney dialysis, etc.).

OPTIONAL: I wish to make additional directives (about life support equipment or other matters):

_____

_____

_____

_____

PLEASE NOTE: If, at some future time, you cannot make decisions for yourself, New York State law prohibits withholding artificial nutrition and hydration from you, unless you have already made your wishes known.

If I cannot eat or drink enough because of my irreversible medical conditions: (☐ I DO) want
☐ I DO NOT
artificial nutrition (intravenous or tube feeding) and hydration (intravenous fluids).

In the absence of my ability to give directions regarding the afore-mentioned life sustaining procedures, it is my intention that this directive shall be honored as the final expression of my legal right to refuse medical treatment and to accept the consequences of such refusal.

I understand the full importance of this directive and I have signed it after thorough consideration of the nature and conse-quences of my refusal of such extraordinary life support proce-dures, including their benefits and disadvantages. This directive is in accordance with my strong convictions and beliefs and is made freely without any inducement or coercion from any person or institution.

_____   _____

SIGNATURE   DATE

I hereby certify that I am over 18 years of age and that I have witnessed the above declarant's signature.

_____   _____

WITNESS   WITNESS

_____   _____

PRINTED WITNESS NAME   PRINTED WITNESS NAME

_____   _____

DATE   DATE

HEALTH CARE PROXY

I, _____ hereby appoint the
following person as my HEALTH CARE AGENT, to make any and all
health care decisions for me except for any restrictions I have
noted below. This Proxy shall take effect when and if I become
unable to make my own health care decisions.

_____   _____

HEALTH CARE AGENT NAME   PHONE

_____

ADDRESS

_____   _____

ALTERNATE HEALTH CARE AGENT NAME   PHONE

_____

ADDRESS

Optional instructions or limitations on the Health Care Agent's
authority, if any:

_____

_____

_____

_____

Unless I revoke it, this Proxy shall remain in effect indefinitely.
(Or until the date or condition stated below, if any.)

_____

_____

PLEASE NOTE: If, at some future time, you cannot make decisions for yourself, New York State law prohibits your Health Care Agent from making decisions about withholding artificial nutrition and hydration from you, unless you have already made your wishes known.

If I cannot eat or drink enough because of my irreversible medical conditions: (☐ I DO ☐ I DO NOT) want artificial nutrition (intravenous or tube feeding) and hydration (intravenous fluids).

_____   _____
SIGNATURE   DATE

_____
ADDRESS

I hereby certify that I am over 18 years of age, and that the person who signed this Proxy appeared to do so willingly and free from duress and that he or she signed (or asked another to sign for him or her) this Proxy in my presence.

_____   _____
WITNESS   WITNESS

_____   _____
PRINTED WITNESS NAME   PRINTED WITNESS NAME

_____   _____
DATE   DATE

BIBLIOGRAPHY

GENERAL

Anonymous. "I've Lost a Kingdom: A victim's remarks on Alzheimer's Disease." *JAGS* 1984;32:935.

Ariès, P. *The Hour of Our Death*. Vintage Books, New York, 1982. Also *The New York Times*, June 14, 1990, p. A6.

Baron, R. J. "An introduction to medical phenomenology: I can't hear you while I'm listening." *Ann. Intern. Med*. 1985;103:606–11.

Beauchamp, T. L., and Perlin, S., eds., *Ethical Issues in Death and Dying*. Englewood Cliffs, N.J.: Prentice-Hall, 1978.

Cassel, E. J. "Informed Consent in the Therapeutic Relationship: Clinical Aspects," in W. T. Reich, ed., *Encyclopedia of Bioethics*, Vol. 2. New York: Free Press, 1978.

———. "The nature of suffering and the goals of medicine." *NEJM* 1982;306:639–45.

Charlson, M. E. "Studies of prognosis: progress and pitfalls." *J. Gen. Intern. Med*. 1987;2:359–61.

Council on Ethical and Judicial Affairs, American Medical Association. "Decisions near the end of life." *JAMA* 1992;267:2229–33.

Diamond, G. A. "Future imperfect: The limitations of clinical prediction models and the limits of clinical prediction." *J. Am. Coll. Cardiol.* 1989;14(3 Suppl. A):12A–22A.

Frankl, V. E. *The Doctor and the Soul: From Psychotherapy to Logotherapy.* New York: Vintage Books, 1955.

———. *Man's Search for Meaning.* 3rd edn. New York: Simon & Schuster, 1984.

Glantz, L. H. "Withholding and withdrawing treatment: The role of criminal law." *Law, Medicine and Health Care* 1987/88;15:231–41.

Glick, S. M. "Humanistic medicine in a modern age." *NEJM* 1981;304:1036–38.

Hastings Center Report. Guidelines on the Termination of Life-Sustaining Treatment and the Care of the Dying. Briarcliff Manor, N.Y.: The Hastings Center, 1987.

Hastings Center Report. "Mercy, murder & morality: Perspectives on euthanasia." Briarcliff Manor, N.Y.: January/February 1989 Supplement, cited hereafter as *Hastings Center Report Suppl.*

Hilden J., and D. F. Habbema. "Prognosis in medicine: An analysis of its meaning and roles." *Theoretical Medicine* 1987;8:349–65.

Hilfiker, D. *Healing the Wounds: A Physician Looks at His Work.* New York: Pantheon Books, 1985.

Illich, I. *Medical Nemesis.* New York: Bantam Books, 1976.

Ingelfinger, F. J. "Informed (but uneducated) consent." *NEJM* 1972;287:465–66.

Kassirer, J. P. "Adding insult to injury: Usurping patients' prerogatives." *NEJM* 1983;308:898–901.

Katz, J. *The Silent World of Doctor and Patient.* New York: Free Press, 1984.

———. "Why doctors don't disclose uncertainty." *Hastings Center Report.* 1984; February, 35–44.

Kleinman, A. *The Illness Narratives: Suffering, Healing and the Human Condition.* New York: Basic Books, 1988.

Kong, A., O. Barnett, F. Mosteller, and C. Youtz. "How medical professionals evaluate expressions of probability." *NEJM* 1986;315:740–44.

Kübler-Ross, E. *On Death and Dying.* New York: Macmillan, 1969.

————. *Working It Through.* New York: Macmillan, 1982.

Lidz, C. W., A. Meisel, M. Osterweis, et al. "Barriers to informed consent." *Ann. Intern. Med.* 1983;99:539–43.

Lipkin, M., T. E. Quill, and R. J. Napodano. "The Medical Interview: A core curriculum for residencies in internal medicine." *Ann. Intern. Med.* 1984;100:277–84.

Lipton, H. L. "Medical care in the last year of life: A review of economic and ethical issues." *Comprehensive Gerontology* (B) 1987;1:89–93.

Mazur, D. J. "Why the goals of informed consent are not realized: Treatise on informed consent for the primary physician." *J. Gen. Int. Med.* 1988;3:370–80.

New York State Task Force on Life and the Law. *Life-Sustaining Treatment: Making Decisions and Appointing a Health Care Agent.* Albany, N.Y., July 1987.

Novack, D. H. "Therapeutic aspects of the clinical encounter." *J. Gen. Intern. Med.* 1987;2:346–55.

Poses, R. M., C. Bekes, I. J. Copare, and W. E. Scott. "The answer to 'What are my chances, doctor?' depends on whom is asked: Prognostic disagreement and inaccuracy for critically ill patients." *Critical Care Medicine* 1989;17:827–33.

Quill, T. E. "Partnerships in patient care: A contractual approach." *Ann. Intern. Med.* 1983;98:228–34.

————. "Recognizing and calibrating to barriers in doctor-patient communication." *Ann. Intern. Med.* 1989;111:51–57.

————, and P. Townsend. "Bad News: Delivery, dialogue and dilemmas." *Arch. Intern. Med.* 1991;151:463–68.

Shelp, E. E. "Courage: A neglected virtue in the patient-physician relationship." *Soc. Sci. Med.* 1984;18:351–60.

————. "Courage and tragedy in clinical medicine." *J. of Medicine and Philosophy* 1983;8:417–29.

Suchman, A. L., and D. A. Matthews. "What makes the doctor-patient relationship therapeutic: Exploring the connexional dimension of medical care." *Ann. Intern. Med.* 1988;108:125–30.

Tolstoy, L. *The Death of Ivan Ilyich.* New York: Bantam Books, 1981.

Tversky, A., and D. Kahneman. "Judgement under uncertainty: Heuristics and biases." *Science* 1974;185:1124–31.

Tversky, A., and D. Kahneman. "The framing of decisions and the psychology of choice." *Science* 1981;211:453–58.

Wanzer, S. H., S. J. Adelstein, R. E. Cranford, et al. "The physician's responsibility toward hopelessly ill patients." *NEJM* 1984;310:955–59.

Wanzer, S. H., D. O. Federman, S. J. Adelstein, et al. "The physician's responsibility toward hopelessly ill patients: A second look." *NEJM* 1989;320:844–49.

Williams, W. C. *The Doctor Stories*. New York: New Directions, 1984.

Worden, J. W. *Grief Counseling and Grief Therapy: A Handbook for the Mental Health Practitioner*. New York: Springer Publishing Co., 1982.

ADVANCE DIRECTIVES

Annas, G. J. "The health care proxy and the living will." *NEJM* 1991; 324:1210–13.

———. "Nancy Cruzan and the right to die." *NEJM* 1990;323:670–73.

Brett, A. S. "Limitations of listing specific medical interventions in advance directives." *JAMA* 1991;266:825–28.

Brunetti, L. L., S. D. Carperos, and R. E. Westlund. "Physicians' attitudes towards living wills and cardiopulmonary resuscitation." *JGIM* 1991;6:323–29.

Curran, W. J. "Defining appropriate medical care: Providing nutrients and hydration for the dying (Law–Medicine notes)." *NEJM* 1985; 313:940–42.

Danis, M., L. Southerland, J. M. Garrett, et al. "A prospective study of advance directives for life-sustaining care." *NEJM* 1991;324:882–88.

Eisendrath, S. J., and A. R. Jonson. "The living will: Help or hindrance?" *JAMA* 1983;249:2054–58.

Emanuel, E. J., and L. L. Emanuel. "Proxy decision making for incompetent patients: An ethical and empirical analysis." *JAMA* 1992;267: 2067–71.

Emanuel, L. L., M. J. Barry, J. D. Stoeckle, et al. "Advance directives for medical care—A case for greater use." *NEJM* 1991;324:889–95.

Greco, P. J., K. A. Schulman, R. Lavizzo-Mourey, and J. Hansen-Flaschen. "The Patient Self-determination Act and the future of advance directives." *Ann. Intern Med.* 1991;115:639–43.

Hare, J., and C. Nelson. "Will outpatients complete living wills? A comparison of two interventions." *J. Gen. Intern. Med.* 1991;6:41–46.

Hospital Association of New York State. *Do Not Resuscitate Orders: Questions and Answers for Health Care Professionals.* Albany, N.Y., September 1990.

Kjellstrand, C. M. "Who should decide about your death?" *JAMA* 1992;267:103–04.

LaPuma, J., D. Orentlicher, and R. J. Moss. "Advance directives on admission: Clinical implications and analysis of the Patient Self-determination Act of 1990." *JAMA* 1991;266:402–05.

Lo, B., and L. Dornbrand. "Guiding the hand that feeds: Caring for the demented elderly." *NEJM* 1984;311:402–04.

———, and F. Rouse. "Family decision-making on trial. Who decides for incompetent patients?" *NEJM* 1990;322:1228–32.

———. "Prisoners of technology: The case of Nancy Cruzan." *NEJM.* 1990;322:1226–32.

Lo, B., and R. Steinbrook. "Beyond the Cruzan case: The U.S. Supreme Court and medical practice." *Ann. Intern. Med.* 1991;114:895–901.

Miles, S. H. "Conflicts between patients' wishes to forgo treatment and the policies of health care facilities." *NEJM* 1989;321:48–50.

———, C. F. Gomez, N. R. Sweibel, and C. K. Cassel. "Nursing Home Policies Addressing the Use or Withdrawal of Life-Sustaining Medical Treatments," in Sweibel and Cassel, eds., *Clinics in Geriatric Medicine: Clinical and Policy Issues in the Care of the Nursing Home Patient,* Vol. 4. Philadelphia: W. B. Saunders, 1988, pp. 681–90.

Miller, T. E. "New York State's health care proxy law." *New York Law Journal,* 1990; vol. 204, no. 32, Aug. 16, 1990, p. 1, col. 1.

Murphy, D. J., and D. B. Matchar. "Life-sustaining therapy: A model for appropriate use." *JAMA* 1990;264:2103–08.

New York State Department of Health and Task Force on Life and the Law. *The Health Care Proxy Law: A Guidebook for Health Care Professionals.* Albany, N.Y., January 1991.

Quill, T. E. "Utilization of nasogastric feeding tubes in a group of chronically ill, elderly patients in a community hospital." *Arch. Int. Med.* 1989;149:1937–41.

Sehgal, A., A. Galbraith, M. Chesney, et al. "How strictly do dialysis patients want their advance directives followed?" *JAMA* 1992;267: 59–63.

Singer, P. A., and M. Siegler. "Advancing the cause of advance directives." *Arch. Intern. Med.* 1992;152:22–24.

Snyder, L. "Life, death and the American College of Physicians: The Cruzan case." *Ann. Intern. Med.* 1990;112:802–04.

Steinbrook, R., and B. Lo. "Artificial feeding—Solid ground, not a slippery slope." *NEJM* 1988;318:286–90.

Tomlinson, T., and H. Brody. "Ethics and communication in do-not-resuscitate orders." *NEJM* 1988;318:43–46.

Uhlmann, R. F., H. Clark, R. A. Pearlman, et al. "Medical management decisions in nursing home patients." *Ann. Intern. Med.* 1987;106: 879–85.

von Preyss-Fredman, S., R. F. Uhlmann, and K. C. Cain. "Physicians' attitudes toward tube feeding chronically ill nursing home patients." *JGIM* 1992;7:46–51.

Weir, R. F., and L. Gostin. "Decisions to abate life-sustaining treatment for nonautonomous patients: Ethical standards and legal liability for physicians after Cruzan." *JAMA* 1990;264:1846–53.

White, B. D., M. Siegler, P. A. Singer, and K. V. Iserson. "What does Cruzan mean to the practicing physician?" *Arch. Intern. Med.* 1991; 151:925–28.

Zweibel, N. R., and C. K. Cassel. "Treatment choices at the end of life: A comparison of decisions by older patients and their physician-selected proxies." *The Gerontologist* 1989;29:615–21.

ASSISTED SUICIDE/VOLUNTARY EUTHANASIA

Abrams, F. R. "Physician participation in assisted suicide." *JAMA* 1990; 263:1197.

Angell, M. "Euthanasia." *NEJM* 1988;319:1348–50.

Anonymous. "It's over, Debbie." *JAMA* 1988;259:272.

Benrubi, G. I. "Euthanasia—The need for procedural safeguards." *NEJM* 1992;326:197–99.

Brahams, D. "Aids in the United States: Education and litigation; the euthanasia debate." *The Lancet* 1988;779–80.

Butler, R. N. "Physician-assisted suicide: The wrong way to go." *Geriatrics* 1990;45:13–14.

Callahan, D. "Can we return death to disease?" in *Hastings Center Report Suppl.*, 4–6.

Cassel, C. K., and D. E. Meier. "Morals and moralism in the debates on euthanasia and assisted suicide." *NEJM* 1990;323:750–52.

Center for Health Ethics and Policy, University of Colorado. "Withholding and withdrawing life-sustaining treatment: A survey of opinions and experiences of Colorado physicians." Graduate School of Public Affairs, Denver, Colorado, May 1988.

Conwell, Y., and E. D. Caine. "Rational suicide and the right to die— Reality and myth." *NEJM* 1991;325:1100–03.

Cundiff, D. *Euthanasia Is Not the Answer: A Hospice Physician's View of the "Death with Dignity" Debate.* Totowa, N.J.: Humana Press, 1992.

Demac, A. R. "Thoughts on physician-assisted suicide." *West. J. Med.* 1988;148:228–30.

Doerflinger, R. "Assisted suicide: Pro-choice or anti-life?" in *Hastings Center Report Suppl.*, 16–19.

Engelhardt, H. T. "Fashioning an ethic for life and death in a postmodern society," in *Hastings Center Report*, 7–9.

Fenigsen, R. "A case against Dutch euthanasia," in *Hastings Center Report Suppl.*, 22–30.

Gaylin, W., L. R. Kass, E. D. Pellegrino, and M. Siegler. "Doctors must not kill." *JAMA* 1988;259·2139–40.

Glantz, L. H. "Withholding and withdrawing treatment: The role of the criminal law." *Law, Medicine & Health Care,* 1987/88;15: 231–41.

Glover, J. *Causing Death and Saving Lives.* New York: Penguin Books, 1977, pp. 182–89.

Goodwin, J. S. "Mercy killing: Mercy for whom?" *JAMA* 1991;265: 326.

Gostin, L. "Drawing a line between killing and letting die: The law and law reform, on medically assisted dying." (pending publication).

The Hemlock Society. "1990 Roper Poll on physician aid-in-dying, allowing Nancy Cruzan to die, and physicians obeying the living will." The Roper Organization, New York, April 24–25, 1990.

————. "1991 Roper Poll of the West Coast on euthanasia." The Roper Organization, New York, May 1991.

Humphry, Derek. *Final Exit.* Secaucus, N.J.: Carol Publishing, 1991.

Initiative 119: The Citizens Initiative for "Yes" on 119 for Death with Dignity. Bellevue, Wash., 1991.

Jackson, D. L., and S. Younger. "Patient autonomy and 'Death with Dignity': Some clinical caveats." *NEJM* 1979;301:404–08.

Jecker, N. S. "Giving death a hand: When the dying and the doctor stand in a special relationship." *JAGS* 1991;39:831–35.

Kamisar, Y. "Some Nonreligious Views Against Proposed 'Mercy Killing' Legislation," in B. M. Leiser, ed., *Values in Conflict: Life, Liberty, and the Rule of Law.* New York: Macmillan, 1981, pp. 109–21.

Kass, L. R. "Neither for love nor money: Why doctors must not kill." *The Public Interest,* Winter 1989;94:25–46.

Koop, C. E. "The challenge of definition," in *Hastings Center Report Suppl.,* 2–3.

Kuhse, H., and P. Singer. "Doctors' practices and attitudes regarding voluntary euthanasia." *Med. J. of Australia* 1988;148:623–727.

Lachs, J. "Humane treatment and the treatment of humans." *NEJM* 1976;294:838–40.

MacIntyre, A. "The Right to Die Garrulously," in R. L. Purtill, ed., *Moral Dilemmas: Readings in Ethics and Social Philosophy.* Belmont, Calif.: Wadsworth, 1985, pp. 129–34.

Meier, D. E., and C. K. Cassel. "Euthanasia in old age: A case study and ethical analysis." *JAGS* 1983;31:294–98.

Meisel, A. "Legal myths about terminating life support." *Arch. Intern. Med.* 1991;151:1497–1502.

Misbin, R. I. "Physicians' aid in dying." *NEJM* 1991;325:1307–11.

National Hemlock Society. *1987 Survey of California Physicians Regarding Voluntary Active Euthanasia for the Terminally Ill.* February 1988.

National Opinion Poll Market Research. *Attitudes Towards Euthanasia among Britain's GPs.* London: NOP Market Research, 1987.

Newman, S. A. "Euthanasia: Orchestrating 'The last syllable of . . . time.' " *University of Pittsburgh Law Review,* Fall 1991;53:153–91.

Orentlicher, D. "Physician participation in assisted suicide." *JAMA* 1989;262:1844–45.

Overmyer, M. "National survey: Physicians' views on the right to die." *Physician Management* 1991;31:40–45.

Parachini, A. "The California humane and dignified death initiative," in *Hastings Center Report Suppl.,* 10–12.

Pearlman, R. A., T. S. Inui, and W. Carter. "Variability in physician bioethical decision making: A case study of euthanasia." *Ann. Intern. Med.* 1982;97:420–25.

Quill, T. E. "Death and dignity: A case of individualized decision making." *NEJM* 1991;324:691–94.

Quill T. E., C. K. Cassel, and D. E. Meier. "Care of the hopelessly ill: Potential clinical criteria for physician-assisted suicide." *NEJM* 1992; 327:1380–84.

Rachels, J. "Active and passive euthanasia." *NEJM* 1975;292:78–80.

Reichel, W., and A. J. Dyck. "Euthanasia: A contemporary moral quandary." *The Lancet* 1989;ii:1321–23.

Richman, J. "The case against rational suicide." *Suicide and Life-Threatening Behavior* 1988:18285–89.

Rigter, H. "Euthanasia in The Netherlands: Distinguishing facts from fiction," in *Hastings Center Report Suppl.,* 31–32.

Rollin, B. *Last Wish.* New York: Linden Press/Simon & Schuster, 1985.

Rouse, F. "Suicide and advance directives," *Hastings Center Report,* 1988; 18:44.

———. "Road to euthanasia or right to refuse care?" *JAMA* 1990;264: 1809.

Singer, P. A., and M. Siegler. "Euthanasia—A critique." *NEJM* 1990; 322:1881–83.

Slovenko, R. "Doctor-assisted suicide." *Med. Law* 1990;9:1006–08.

Teno, J., and J. Lynn. "Voluntary active euthanasia: The individual case and public policy." *JAGS* 1991;39:827–30.

Vaux, K. L. "Debbie's dying: Mercy killing and the good death." *JAMA* 1988;259:2140–41.

Voluntary Active Euthanasia. "AGS Public Policy Committee." *JAGS* 1991;39:826.

Weir, R. F. "The morality of physician-assisted suicide." *Law, Medicine, and Health Care,* Spring–Summer 1992;20:116–25.

Wilson, W. C., N. G. Smedira, C. Fink, et al. "Ordering and administration of sedatives and analgesics during the withholding and withdrawal of life support from critically ill patients." *JAMA* 1992;267: 949–53.

Wolf, S. M. "Holding the line on euthanasia," in *Hastings Center Report Suppl.,* 13–15.

———. "Final Exit: The end of argument." *Hastings Center Report,* 1992;22:30–33.

Comfort Care/Hospice

Broadfield, L. "Evaluation of palliative care: Current status and future directions." *J. of Palliative Care* 1988;4:21–28.

Dobratz, M. C., R. Wade, L. Herbst, and T. Ryndes. "Pain efficacy in home hospice patients. A longitudinal study." *Cancer Nursing* 1991; 14:20–26.

Garfield, C. A. *Psychosocial Care of the Dying Patient.* New York: McGraw-Hill, 1978.

Godkin, M. A., M. J. Krant, and N. J. Doster. "The impact of hospice care on families." *Intl. J. Psychiatry in Medicine* 1983–84;13:153–65.

Rhymes, J. "Hospice care in America." *JAMA* 1990;264:369–72.

Seale, C. F. "What happens in hospices: A review of research evidence." *Soc. Sci. Med.* 1989;28:551–59.

Stoddard, S. "Hospice in the United States: An overview." *J. of Palliative Care* 1989;5:10–19.

Teno, J. M., V. Mor, and J. Fleishman. "Preferences of HIV-infected patients for aggressive versus palliative care." *NEJM* 1991;324:1140.

Volicer, L., Y. Rheaume, J. Brown, et al. "Hospice approach to the treatment of patients with advanced dementia of the Alzheimer type." *JAMA* 1986;256:2210–13.

Wallston, K. A., C. Burger, R. A. Smith, and R. J. Baugher. "Comparing the quality of death for hospice and non-hospice cancer patients." *Medical Care* 1988;26:177–82.

Zimmerman, J. M. *Hospice: Complete Care for the Terminally Ill.* Baltimore: Urban & Schwarzenberg, 1981.

DISCONTINUING DIALYSIS

Campbell, J. D., and A. R. Campbell. "The social and economic costs of end-stage renal disease: A patient's perspective." *NEJM* 1978;299:386–92.

Evans, R. W., D. L. Manninen, L. P. Garrison, et al. "The quality of life of patients with end-stage renal disease." *NEJM* 1985;312:553–59.

Holley, J. L., T. E. Finucane, and A. H. Moss. "Dialysis patients' attitudes about cardiopulmonary resuscitation and stopping dialysis." *Am. J. Nephrol.* 1989;9:245–51.

Kolata, G. B. "Dialysis after nearly a decade." *Science* 1980;208:473–76.

Motes, C. E. "Discontinuation of dialysis." *ANNA Journal* 1989;16:413–15.

Neu, S., and C. M. Kjellstrand. "Stopping long-term dialysis. An empirical study of withdrawal of life-supporting treatment." *NEJM* 1986;314:14–20.

Port, F. K., R. A. Wolfe, V. M. Hawthorne, and C. W. Ferguson. "Discontinuation of dialysis therapy as a cause of death. *Am. J. Nephrol.* 1989;9:145–49.

Roberts, J. C., and C. M. Kjellstrand. "Choosing death: Withdrawal from chronic dialysis without medical reason." *Acta Med. Scand.* 1988;223:181–86.

Roberts, J. C., R. Snyder, and C. M. Kjellstrand. "Withdrawing life support—The survivors." *Acta Med. Scand.* 1988;224:141–48.

PROGNOSIS AND AGING

Avorn, J. "Benefit and cost analysis in geriatric care: Turning age discrimination into health policy." *NEJM* 1984;310:1294–1300.

Broadfield, L. "Evaluation of palliative care: Current status and future directions." *J. of Palliative Care* 1988;4:21–28.

Carlson, R. W., L. Devich, and R. R. Frank. "Development of a comprehensive supportive care team for the hopelessly ill on a university hospital medical service." *JAMA* 1988;259:378–83.

Charlson, M. E. "Studies of prognosis: Progress and pitfalls." *JGIM* 1987;2:359–61.

Diamond, G. A. "Future Imperfect: The limitations of clinical prediction models and the limits of clinical prediction." *J. Am. Coll. Cardiol.* 1989;14:12A–22A.

Fries, J. F. "Aging, natural death and the compression of morbidity." *NEJM* 1980;303:130–35.

Hilden, J., and J. D. F. Habbema. "Prognosis in medicine: An analysis of its meaning and roles." *Theoretical Medicine* 1987;8:349–65.

Olshansky, S. J., B. A. Carnes, and C. Cassel. "In search of Methuselah: Estimating the upper limits to human longevity." *Science* 1990;250:634–40.

Olshansky, S. J., M. A. Rudberg, B. A. Carnes, C. K. Cassel, and J. A. Brody. "Trading off longer life for worsening health: The expansion of morbidity hypothesis." *J. of Aging and Health* 1991;3:194–216.

Poses, R. M., C. Bekes, F. J. Copare, and W. E. Scott. "The answer to 'What are my chances, doctor?' depends on whom is asked: Prognostic disagreement and inaccuracy for critically ill patients." *Crit. Care. Med.* 1989;17:827–33.

Schonwetter, R. S., T. A. Teasdale, P. Storey, and R. J. Luchi. "Estimation of survival time in terminal cancer patients: An impedance to hospice admissions?" *The Hospice Journal* 1990;6:65–79.

RESUSCITATION IN THE ELDERLY

Bedell, S. E., et al. "DNR orders for critically-ill patients in the hospital." *JAMA* 1986;256:233–37.

Braithwaite, S., and D. C. Thomasina. "New guidelines on foregoing life-sustaining treatment in incompetent patients: An anti-cruelty policy." *Ann. Intern. Med.* 1986;104:711–15.

Council on Scientific Affairs and Council on Ethical and Judicial Affairs. "Persistent vegetative state and the decision to withdraw or withhold life support." *JAMA* 1990;263:426–30.

Hilfiker, D. "Allowing the debilitated to die." *NEJM* 1983, 308:716–19.

Lipton, H. L. "DNR decisions in a community hospital." *JAMA* 1986, 256:1164–69.

Lo, B., and A. R. Jonsen. "Ethical decisions in the care of a patient terminally ill with metastatic cancer." *Ann. Intern. Med.* 1980;92:107–11.

———. "Clinical decisions to limit treatment." *Ann. Intern. Med.* 1980;93:764–68.

New York State Task Force on Life and the Law. *Do Not Resuscitate Orders: The Proposed Legislation and Report of the New York State Task Force on Life and the Law.* 2nd edn. New York, N.Y., August 1988.

Perkins, H. S. "Ethics at the end of life: Practical principles for making resuscitation decisions." *J. Gen. Intern. Med.* 1986;1:170–76.

Quill, T. E., and N. M. Bennett. "The effects of a hospital policy and state legislation on resuscitation orders for geriatric patients." *Arch. Intern. Med.* 1992;152:569–72.

Quill, T. E., J. A. Stankaitis, and C. R. Krause. "The effect of a community hospital resuscitation policy on elderly patients." *New York State Journal of Medicine,* December 1986, 622–25.

Schmale, A. H., and W. B. Patterson. "Comfort Care Only—Treatment Guidelines for the Terminal Patient," in C. A. Garfield, ed., *Psychosocial Care of the Dying Patient.* New York: McGraw-Hill, 1978.

Schneiderman, L. J., and R. G. Spragg. "Ethical decisions in discontinuing mechanical ventilation." *NEJM* 1988;318:984–88.

Steinbock, B. "The removal of Mr. Herbert's feeding tube." *Hastings Center Report,* October 1983;13–22.

Suber, D. G., and W. J. Tabor. "Withholding of life-sustaining treatment from the terminally ill, incompetent patient: Who decides?" Part I. *JAMA* 1982;248:2250–51.

Volicer, L., et al., "Hospice approach to the treatment of patients with advanced dementia of the Alzheimer's type." *JAMA* 1986, 256:2210–13.

SUICIDE

Allenbeck, P., C. Bolund, and G. Ringback. "Increased suicide rate in cancer patients." *J. Clin. Epidemiol.* 1989;42:611–16.

Breitbart, W. "Suicide in cancer patients." *Oncology* 1987;1:49–55.

Conwell, Y., and E. D. Caine. "Rational suicide and the right to die: Reality and myth." *NEJM* 1991;325:1100–03.

Finnerty, J. L. "Ethics in rational suicide." *Crit. Care Nurs. Qu.* 1987; 10:86–90.

Hall, Joanne M., and P. E. Stevens. "AIDS: A guide to suicide assessment." *Arch. Psychiatric Nursing.* 1988;2:115–20.

Hjortsjo, T. "Suicide in relation to somatic illness and complications." *Crisis* 1987;8/2:125–37.

Humphry, D. "Letter to the Editor: The case for rational suicide." *Suicide and Life-threatening Behavior* 1987;17:335–38.

Kliban, M. G. "Suicide and the hospice patient." *Am. J. Hospice Care* 1987:15–21.

MacKenzie, T. B., and M. K. Popkin. "Suicide in the medical patient." *Intl. J. Psychiatry in Medicine* 1987;17:3–22.

Monk, M. "Epidemiology of suicide." *Epidemiologic Reviews* 1987;9:-51–69.

Perlin, S., ed. *A Handbook for the Study of Suicide.* New York: Oxford University Press, 1975.

Rangell, L. "The decision to terminate one's life: Psychoanalytic thoughts on suicide." *Suicide and Life-threatening Behavior* 1988;18: 28–46.

Snipe, R. M. "Ethical issues in the assessment and treatment of a rational suicidal client." *The Counseling Psychologist* 1988;16:128–38.

Szasz, T. "The case against suicide prevention." *Am. Psychologist* 1986; 41:806–12.

Weber, W. M. "Letter to the Editor: What right to die?" *Suicide and Life-threatening Behavior* 1988;18:181–96.

THE NETHERLANDS

Anonymous. "Final report of the Netherlands State Commission on euthanasia: An English summary." *Bioethics* 1987;1:163–74.

Brahams, D. "Euthanasia in the Netherlands." *The Lancet* 1990;335: 591–92.

Gomez, C. F. *Regulating Death: Euthanasia and the Case of the Netherlands.* New York: Free Press, 1991.

Leenen, H. J. J. "Coma patients in the Netherlands." *Brit. Med. J.* 1990;300:69.

Pence, G. E. "Do not go slowly into that dark night: Mercy killing in Holland." *Am. J. of Med.* 1988;84:139–41.

Rigter, H., E. Borst-Eilers, and N. J. J. Leenan. "Euthanasia across the North Sea." *Brit. Med. J.* 1988; 1594.

van der Maas, P. J., et al. "Euthanasia and other medical decisions concerning the end of life." *The Lancet* 1991;338:669–74.

INDEX

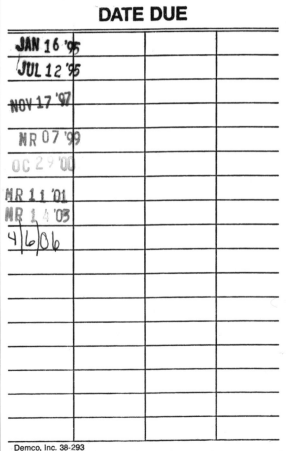